PRAISE FOR *THE HEARTBREAK YEARS*

"If *The Heartbreak Years* were a person, it'd be the girl you meet in line for the bathroom at the club. Vulnerable, hilarious, there to whisper hard-earned wisdom into your ear while holding back your hair. Minda Honey has written a fierce rallying cry for the single and lovesick, for those who dare to see the hope in being a romantic. The stories in this book are vibrant, tender, self-aware without being jaded, compulsively readable but never easy. When some f'boy has got you down, Honey's words are an outstretched hand reaching to lift you back up."

—Edgar Gomez, author of *High-Risk Homosexual* and *Alligator Tears*

"Every few decades, there's that one book that shapes directly how we all understand the potentially radical, and radically heartbreaking, space between touching and being touched, running to and running away, f'ing shit up and feeling f'ed. Minda Honey has created a momentous piece of art, of course, but most importantly, *The Heartbreak Years* will teach a generation of us what's possible when writing through, to, and beneath the pulpy inside of desire and fear. I'm so thankful. Motherf'ers finna be reading the f out of this book."

—Kiese Laymon, bestselling author of *Long Division* and *Heavy*

THE
HEART
BREAK
YEARS

THE
HEART
BREAK
YEARS

A MEMOIR

MINDA
HONEY

Little
a

Published by Little A, New York

www.apub.com

Amazon, the Amazon logo, and Little A are trademarks of Amazon.com, Inc., or its
affiliates.

ISBN-13: 9781662500022 (hardcover)
ISBN-13: 9781662500015 (paperback)
ISBN-13: 9781662500008 (digital)

Cover design by Emily Mahon

Cover image: © Melpomenem / Getty; © Globe Turner, © PHOTOARTDESIGN,
© Hitdelight, © EVorona / Shutterstock

Printed in the United States of America

First edition

For the women who made me:
Minda, Lucy Ann, Melinda, Jasmine, and Ryeshia

Is the Colosseum beautiful because it's
destroyed or because it's still standing?
—Chet'la Sebree, *Field Study*

CONTENTS

AUTHOR'S NOTE

I have changed many details, names, and defining characteristics, and I have been intentionally vague in several instances to give grace, make space for the failure of memory, and acknowledge that this is a singular point of view on several moments in time that belong to the perspectives of many. Still, this is my Truth.

PART I: HOPE

Chapter 1

The Real Orange County

2008: great year for Obama, trash year for Minda.

It was a time before Tinder, before Uber, before Amazon same-day delivery. I had a Yahoo! email address and a Razr flip phone on a plan so basic I couldn't send or receive photos. I'd never known the shock—or awe—of an unsolicited dick pic. It was the year an inspiring young presidential candidate campaigning on a platform for change captivated the nation. A political message I should have embraced on a personal level: At twenty-three, I was still dating my high school boyfriend and driving the same car I'd had since senior year. More than a year after I'd graduated from college, I continued to do the same prospectless work I'd supposedly gotten a degree to avoid. The previous year, I'd failed at my first Big Girl Job—rather, I was sabotaged into quitting.

It was the kind of corporate environment that considered crying in the restroom a badge of honor. And I was maxed out on coded stories from my manager about how "people" who lived downtown wore hoodies in the summertime to hide their guns. Absurd. So, when that racist manager took me to lunch and, over a Panera Pick Two, strongly urged me to quit, I accepted her invitation, then finished my soup and sandwich.

For the job that was supposed to launch my career, my high school sweetheart and I had relocated to Cincinnati, Ohio—a little more than an hour north of where we'd grown up in Louisville, Kentucky. Cincy hadn't been good for us or our relationship. Typical couple shit—money problems exacerbated by the hotheadedness of young love. Tyler was making almost nothing as a ballroom dance instructor, so I grudgingly worked two low-paying hourly jobs to replace the salary of the job I'd quit. Our lease was ending; we knew we would not be staying. And just as we were asking ourselves *What's next?*, his grandparents put the word out that they needed house sitters for their home in Orange County, California. We volunteered. Tyler could pursue his dream of becoming a professional dancer. And I, unsure of what I wanted to do career-wise, was just content to flee the cold.

I've always hated winter. My dad used to turn on the Weather Channel first thing every morning. I'd spoon instant oatmeal into my mouth while watching weeks of freezing temps, cloudy days, rain, rain, rain as the weatherman worked his way across the country, arm stretched against the restraints of his suit jacket, until he reached the West Coast. There, the days were populated with little yellow suns and temperatures warm enough to never need a coat. It seemed unfair. How could this golden dream be real life, and why would anyone choose to live anywhere else?

Tyler and I spent the months before our move to California back in Louisville with friends and family. In May, we loaded up my little red Jetta for our road trip. I decided to leave my socks behind. I wouldn't need them where we were headed. We didn't own a GPS unit—they were still a luxury—and neither one of us could read a road atlas. So, we printed directions from MapQuest.com and followed each numbered turn and exit carefully from state to state, pitching crumpled-up sheets of paper into the back seat as we went.

In Louisville, Tyler had stayed with his mom, and I with mine. After months of living separately, we were ready to resume the rhythm of daily life together. Time and absence had made the small interior of the car feel more expansive than our two-bedroom Cincinnati apartment. We were hopeful.

Along the road, the water maples I'd grown up with—knotty-rooted trees that shot up fast in the lawn of my childhood home—gave way to Missouri oak trees with scalloped leaves. Oklahoma brought a golden haze of prairies that whirred past the car windows, then spread, thinned, and disappeared into the flatlands of Texas, all dirt and desert studded with prickly pear cacti.

Cruising down a long tract of nowhere across the Panhandle, Tyler was pulled over for speeding. The officer ran our plates and then motioned for my boyfriend to join him in the front seat of his cop car for a chat. Nervous, I watched them in the rearview mirror. When Tyler came back, he refused to tell me what the officer had said. We continued down the highway while I wondered if the cop had lectured him about what white boys shouldn't be doing with Black girls.

In Arizona, there were saguaros standing tall with their arms raised skyward. To reach Sedona, we traveled through a dense forest of red-barked Ponderosa pines. We drove with the windows down, in the coolness of the trees' shade, breathing in their sweet butterscotch scent. The mixtapes of emo love songs I'd burned for Tyler in high school played on repeat—the soundtrack to our young romance and now our journey westward. We argued. Over his insistence that five dollars wasn't too much to pay for a bottle of Coke with lunch. And again when I refused to frolic in a creek with my frog giggin', deer huntin', semicountry boy—"You don't know what could be living in that water!" I wailed. The disagreements continued as we pitched our tent in Carrizozo, New Mexico, near hardened lava flow.

In Las Vegas, we just knew we were witnessing a sliver of Tyler's future as we watched Cirque du Soleil dancers bound from one end of the stage to the other, glide through the air, and induce as much reverence as a savior walking on water.

As we cut an arc around the outer edge of the Mojave Desert on I-15, just after we'd crossed from Nevada into California, I pointed out the window at the short, sprouting candelabras. The Mormons had named them "Joshua trees." Then the luggage carrier on the top of my car flew open, and a pillow slid down the windshield. I whipped the car to the side of the road, and we got out. Concerned for my safety, Tyler yelled at me to stay put as he sprinted into the freeway to collect sheets and shirts and other runaway possessions. The wind snatched at my sundress. Truck drivers watched Tyler hop in and out of traffic and slowed their big rigs down to hold the other cars at bay.

Palm trees tall enough to dust the sky ushered us west toward the ocean. In a neighborhood across from a golf course, his grandparents' backyard had a lemon tree, three orange trees, and a fig tree. The fruit from their neighbor's grapefruit tree hung fat and heavy over their shared fence. Sweet abundance.

This was Orange County.

Chapter 2

FLOUNDERING

We arrived in May. The understanding was that we'd find work, save up, and move into a place of our own before Tyler's grandparents returned in December. Tyler got a job at Disneyland. He was tall enough, certainly charming enough, to be a prince but not quite broad-shouldered enough. He was lanky, more likely to be—and likely more interested in being—cast in an excellent adventure alongside Bill and Ted than to kiss a Sleeping Beauty. So, he ran some ride that required him to dress like a futuristic car mechanic. The gig was part time, which allowed him to attend a community dance school that had granted him a partial scholarship. Some nights, after his shift was over, we'd head back up to the park, enter for free, and watch the night parade, characters and floats lit up in LEDs. "One day," Tyler would say dreamily as dancers in intricate costumes pranced past the crowd. It was a moment made for being the Good Girlfriend—squeezing his shoulder, offering a reassuring smile. But generally, I'd just stand there trying to figure out how someone could spend all day at an amusement park and then have any interest in returning off the clock. Children dreaming. Tyler dreaming. Me restless and ready to leave.

I'd graduated college during the Great Recession, and the well-paying, entry-level office positions my generation had been promised in exchange for our degrees were nearly nonexistent. In Orange County, I was forced to fall back on the retail skills I'd developed working mall jobs in high school. A department store hired me to sell skin-care creams and masks.

Being back in retail—hourly work at all, really—felt demeaning. Throughout my entire education, I'd been taught to believe that if you didn't go to college, you'd be trapped in low-wage jobs, serving up french fries, cleaning up other people's filth, or being on your feet for long hours. To motivate the youth of America, both the work and the workers had been shamed. They deserved disrespect and minimal pay because they hadn't applied themselves. Did we want to be them? No. Well then, get good grades and go to college. And don't graduate into the biggest recession of the last century, and don't even think about how race, gender, class, and citizenship factor into any of it. Not that they were ever far from my mind.

My father had been in the air force. He met my mother while stationed in the Philippines. It was his service that had made it possible for him to drag our family into the middle class—which we were, no matter how precarious that status was during certain stretches of my childhood. Through his veterans' benefits, my father secured a mortgage on a home in the suburbs, and he attended college for free. As the daughter of a Black veteran and a Filipino immigrant, I was aware of the sacrifices my parents had made in hopes my life would be easier than theirs. A mall job could not be the culmination of their dreams for me.

I treated the cosmetics position as if I were just passing through. My shame wouldn't allow me to be truly thankful for it, even in a tight job market. When people back home asked me what I was doing out in Cali, I hated telling them. I struggled to reorient my understanding of who I was in a way that didn't conflict with being a college graduate working retail. I was no longer receiving societal accolades as a high-achieving student, and my career trajectory was not soaring along as I'd imagined it would post-graduation. Even though the news was there to assure me *It's not you; it's the economy,* I still put it on me. I still blamed myself for failing to be an exception.

It'd be easy to read my too-good-for-retail mentality as the hubris of youth, but it was more than that. One overtly racist manager in Cincinnati had rerouted my entire career. There are white former peers of mine who began in the position I had and are now senior executives within the same corporation I was pushed out of. I'd felt like a failure for quitting when asked to, but the only thing I'd failed at was the not-so-small task of succeeding in the face of racism. And for what? To prove I could write a stellar press release under mental and emotional duress? But the fact that I'd left and was unable to find similar employment elsewhere made me question whether what my manager had said about me was true—I didn't belong. I was unworthy. She'd stolen more than just a job, more than just a career from me. She'd hijacked my sense of self-worth. Instead of spending my twenties figuring out what I'd actually like to do for work, I spent those years fixated on finding my way back to corporate America, just so I could prove to myself, and others, what was already known: she was wrong. It would be many years before—heartbroken in Denver on one of the first warm days of spring—I'd turn loose that resentment, and everything else that came with it, so that I could be free, free to reach out for what I really wanted.

With Tyler mostly at work or in dance classes, I was eager to make new friends, which is not easy as an adult. You can't coast up alongside someone else's cart at the grocery store and be like, "Oh, you like Cap'n Crunch? Me too! Wanna kick it?" Coworkers were an obvious start, but the other beauty-counter girls were so cool I immediately turned into a Kentucky bumpkin in their presence. It took me more than a week to realize the unofficial uniform was all-black everything. I was either dressed too stuffy in a collared shirt and pressed skirt or too casual in a short sundress. I envied the girls' perfectly lined eyes and bold lips. They had the camaraderie of a crew who'd been working together for years.

What we sold was expensive, but beauty has always come at a cost for women—monetary, emotional, both. Several of my coworkers would go on to more prestigious counters, regional roles, or working directly for the brands we represented. And some would even become makeup artists to celebrities. But I was oblivious to the potential career progression of the work we did, looking down in shame as they headed up toward their dreams. I had dreams, too, but I wasn't paying them any attention. The desire to be a writer has forever flickered inside me, but at that time, I took it about as seriously as my aspirations at seven years old to become a firefighter–TV chef–ballerina. While in Orange County, I did find a writing group on Meetup.com. I was decades younger than everyone else and the only Black writer. Still, over time, I did manage to form a cross-generational friendship with an older writer.

In the department store break room, I'd sit alone and watch as the other girls crowded around a single table, gossiping about customers or that super-tall hot dude who worked in Shoes. Eventually, they began to warm up to me. It'd probably taken a while—thanks to my attitude about the job—for them to figure out whether I was stuck-up, standoffish, or just shy. Idle on a slow night, someone would marvel at how clear my skin was—"You don't wear foundation?"—and another would offer to show me how to apply gel liner with a brush. I'd get invited to one-dollar taco night at El Torito, listen to their boyfriend woes, share my own. But by the time I could consider myself one of the girls, I'd already given my notice—I was going to work for an eccentric millionaire's one-man branding agency. I stayed in touch with a few of the women, but I was no longer part of the tight department store ecosystem. The new job was a pay cut and still hourly, but I saw it as a résumé builder and an ego boost—one step closer to regaining the career I'd lost.

In Louisville, Tyler and I had mostly shared the same friends. At that age, in a city that size, there was the strong sense that everyone knew everyone—if you showed up at a house party with a bottle, no matter how cheap, you were immediately good with us and everyone else in attendance. My best friend's boyfriend became Tyler's best friend, the two launching a break-dancing crew. Dudes who wanted to get with me in college abandoned the chase after meeting him, all of us somehow becoming pals.

But that wasn't going to be the case in Orange County. His coworkers made their money smiling for the Mouse and had a kind of purity about them that made me feel like a goth kid at Vacation Bible School. The dance kids treated me like an outsider because I'm not a dancer—I don't even have enough rhythm to confidently do the Electric Slide at weddings. Between work and dance classes, there wasn't much time for Tyler to spend with me. And after lengthy shifts at the department store, the last thing I wanted to do was walk around an amusement park. Tyler had little interest in spending time with the makeup-counter girls. And on the rare evening we were both home, I declined invitations to rewatch action movies he loved; instead, I spent hours reading popular new feminist blogs like *Jezebel*.

This separation of social circles had begun in Cincy. Back then, I'd been working too much to feel any kind of way about it. In Orange County, though, with no friend group of my own to distract me from his, I had plenty of time to measure the distance between us, note how and who we spent our time with, and worry about our increasingly diverging interests.

I figured if I could sell a couch on Craigslist, why couldn't I find a bestie there? My middle sister laughed at me, accurately asserting that it wasn't my greatest idea. Still, I made a post. I met up with one girl who'd messaged me—at the mall. She'd clearly lied about her age and was much younger than me. Her foundation was so thick it looked like she'd smeared peanut butter on her face. After walking a few laps around the mall, she asked me to give her a ride to a friend's house, where some guy they knew was going to tattoo her in the garage.

"I don't know if the lighting in a garage is good enough for a tattoo," I cautioned her.

"You're right." She stopped walking for a second. "We should do it in the kitchen." I left without giving her a lift anywhere.

I met up with another girl at a hookah lounge. She had an extra ticket to a music festival and promised me that if I went with her, she'd buy the drugs. I hadn't entered my Doing Drugs with Strangers era yet, so I politely declined.

I didn't see either girl again.

Then, on the same website where I'd found my writing group, I saw a meetup for twentysomething girls who lived in Orange County. My first outing with the group was dinner at a midscale chain restaurant. I sat next to a Black girl who'd moved from Nebraska and had a little diamond tattooed behind her ear. I liked her, and some of the other girls, enough to keep coming back. The group had dozens of members. Most of them early twenties, most of them transplants, and most of them recently single. A lot of them were in those years following graduation, looking at the boy they'd dated through college, sometimes longer, and wondering how he was going to fit into their future. Some girls were single because their exes spent hours marathoning video games in dark rooms, with no interest in getting out of the house. Some were single because their exes spent recklessly on their hobbies while their girlfriends were mulling over retirement plans for the first time. And some girls *should have been* single because their exes couldn't be trusted to have big, important conversations with them.

I knew, between the two of us, Tyler and I were not earning enough to move out of his grandparents' house. I'd checked out the apartments on Craigslist while cruising for besties. Weekly, I pushed him to speak to them about letting us stay longer. I reminded him and he forgot, and I reminded him again. Summer became fall, if only in name. The weather hardly changes in Southern California. The week of Halloween, Tyler told me he'd spoken to his grandparents. They'd said no. Sharing a home with an unwed couple went against their values.

When I asked him what *we* were going to do, he said *he* was going to stay. I was irate. I wanted us to move out together. He accused me of attempting to ruin his fledgling dance career. For his eighteenth birthday, when he was a senior in high school and I was a freshman in college, I'd purchased his first dance classes. A year later, I arranged it so his break-dance crew could practice in the basement of my college dorm, even though he wasn't a student. In Cincy, I'd supported us while he'd made no money as a ballroom dance instructor. I'd happily headed west with him without any clear personal purpose. On days I didn't pack his lunch, he forgot to eat and returned home from work and dance class dizzy and exhausted.

His accusation was undeserved, but his assessment of the situation wasn't untrue. He really couldn't work any more than he already was. While I was in college, he'd put in time at miserable jobs like credit-card call centers and predawn shifts at factories. His life in Louisville had such an aimlessness to it, there hadn't been any doubt that when I accepted the offer in Cincinnati, he'd trail after me. I'd grown accustomed to his life lived in deference to mine and my vision for our life together. *I* was the one doing serious things, the one with a future, the one applying myself. Orange County changed all that. A path toward the dance dream he'd always held but never knew how to follow was appearing before him. As I grappled with belonging and was lost in career uncertainty about who I was and what I wanted to be, Tyler was coming into himself. He'd found community and was nourishing his passion.

"This has me torn up," he said in our dark bedroom, leaning against the closet door. "I've been trying to find a way to tell you for months."

Months? I sat on the bed, the hall light cutting in through the open bedroom door isolating me from the darkness. He'd known I couldn't stay since August. Which meant every time I'd asked him to talk to his grandparents, he'd known their answer and he'd lied. He was why I only had a month's notice to move out. I thought about how, had he told me sooner, I could have saved more; we could have planned together.

Our relationship had spanned six years. Was this the end? Tyler didn't want to break up. But I wasn't sure I wanted to stay together. I did know that I didn't want to be alone in California. It'd been six months since I'd been in Kentucky, the longest I'd ever stayed away from home. And Orange County was the farthest I'd ever been. Three time zones separated me and everyone else I loved. Their lives were progressing ahead of mine, like I was chasing them through their day, eating breakfast as they were eating lunch, staring at the clock at work while they were clocking out and heading home.

But wasn't I already alone if Tyler and I weren't making big life decisions together? I didn't know how to have a future with a boy who didn't know how to tell me things, important things, major things. Who hadn't even *tried* to tell me. Who left me to deal with the consequences of not knowing on my own. This time, he hadn't even given me a chance to play the Supportive Girlfriend. To say, *Don't worry—we'll figure it out.* I loved him. He was kind, talented; he knew himself. But what would our future look like? Would it be me bailing water while he tried to hide the hole in our ship, snug in his life vest?

My own life was becoming unrecognizable to me. New city, new job, new friends . . . New boyfriend? I wasn't sure if I'd stay or leave California—if I'd stay or leave Tyler. And I only had a few weeks to decide.

Chapter 3

SAFE HARBOR

Before Tyler, there was a boy whose name sang with alliteration fit for a newscaster. I was sixteen and a half, more than half my lifetime ago. I was gone off this boy who lived around the corner from me. He was two grades ahead in school—a senior—and we rode the bus together. Tall, Black, beautiful in that stony, delicate way only young men can be. He was already toxic, poisoned by his father, knuckles split, scarred from fighting. One morning, on the ride to school, he showed me a picture of his girlfriend, his other hand in my lap, beneath my uniform skirt. "You should shave," he said. I listened.

In the afternoon, on the walk to his house—I'd pass mine and double back later, just to spend more time with him—the younger boys would crowd around, their white school shirts untucked, sneakers untied. They wanted to hear stories about his fights. They wanted to know if he'd play basketball with them. They were gone off him, too. We knew something special when we saw it. When he smiled, his cheekbones rode high, and his eyes stretched into slits as thin as pennies.

Once, when it was just the two of us, the younger boys somewhere else that afternoon, he looked down at me walking alongside him. My backpack straps dug into my shoulders, weighed down by AP textbooks.

He said, "You're going to be pretty one day when you get those braces off and stop hunching over like that." Again, I listened, standing up straighter beneath the weight.

Another day, school out for the summer, I walked around the corner to his house, alone, and into the boy's living room. The front door clicked shut behind me. I left without my virginity. It was over before I'd even understood what we'd begun. Afterward, he turned on BET and pointed out which girls in the music videos he thought were fine.

Back then, there wasn't a consent culture. There were just fast-tailed girls who let their hearts race places their bodies didn't belong. Girls who wanted it, like I'd wanted it. But not yet. Not like that. Wanting is a welcome mat for danger. There is no safe place for PG-13 lust, for innocent desires. For girls, there was "Just say no." And for boys, like the boy who lived around the corner from me, there was "Just the tip." Only girls didn't know it was a game designed for us to lose. And who would want to play a game like that more than once?

The next time, I said, "I don't think we should . . ." The next time, there were no games, just rape. He didn't listen.

He had a problem with taking things that didn't belong to him. The last I heard, one of his friends told me he had a baby on the way and had been locked up for pulling a gun on a pizza delivery guy at his own apartment. It wasn't hard for the police to figure out where to find him. Who knows if it's true, but when I google his newscaster name, a name he shares with many men, the only link relevant to him is a Florida mug shot from around the same time for an out-of-state felony charge.

He doesn't look stony, delicate, beautiful. He doesn't look like anything to me. He's wearing a white shirt, just like in the picture of him I still have in a box full of high school keepsakes under my bed. That photo had been taken when he still looked like something special. I don't ever look at it, but I've never been able to let it go, either.

Tyler felt safe.

In the notebooks my best friends and I passed back and forth during class, I wrote that he was "cute" but that he was a year younger than me, and I was after older boys with cars and money for dates. When a friend saw us together in the hallway, she teased, "Where'd you find him? Baby Gap?"

Still, I kept my books in Tyler's locker. I brought him to homecoming. Drove him home after school. On the news, the politicians charging our country into war were mostly older, mostly male, mostly white. At home, I abided by the rules of my father. But I found that with Tyler, I made the decisions.

I became the more experienced woman to a slightly younger man's shy adoration. I waited with anticipation for his slow-moving sexual advances, exploring those earliest pleasures at my own pace with no pressure. Even when Tyler did eagerly leap ahead, like plunging a hand down my pants mid-movie on an afternoon when we had cut class with our friends, he was easily redirected and respectfully retreated whenever I seemed uncertain.

Tyler offered protection. After repeatedly witnessing creepy older men approach me while I pumped gas, a situation I couldn't flee until my tank filled, he volunteered to permanently take over the task for me while I remained seated behind the wheel.

In college, I started drinking a few months shy of my twenty-first birthday. That's not true. Not completely. I didn't just start *drinking*; I started binge drinking. The first time I called Tyler while drunk to come see me at my dorm, he said, "No. I don't like drunk girls." But that didn't stop me from drinking.

Although I'd started dating Tyler in high school, it took a drunken night at a friend's house party to tell him about the boy who'd lived around the corner from me. Five years had passed since the boy hadn't listened, had held me down, had taken what wasn't his, and I'd never said a word about it to anyone. I don't remember a whole lot from the night in college when I told Tyler—just sitting in a dark corner, leaning into the safe harbor of my boyfriend's shoulder, sobbing to him over and over again, "I don't know why he did that to me."

"That's his problem, not yours. He's the one with the problem," Tyler said.

He was twenty then. Today, I see grown men who can't call out other men. They give nothing but grace to offensive men. They're men who want to make excuses. Men who say, "Well, I wasn't there. How do we know what really happened?"; "What did *she* do, though?"; "Why'd she even go over there, then?" Who say everything except, "He's the one with the problem." He's the one with the problem. *He's the one with the problem.*

Maybe that's why even though I knew what Tyler said was true, I didn't know what to do with that truth. Why that truth didn't make me feel any different the next morning. Why I let the boy from around the corner's problem continue to be my problem for years.

Tyler didn't like drunk girls—that was true—and he didn't like having sex with me when I was drunk. "It's the only time you want to," he said in bed in our first apartment together, the one in the old Victorian house that got broken into twice. If the language had existed then, he might have said that what he wanted was ongoing enthusiastic consent. But he didn't have those words. All he knew was drunk sex didn't feel right to him. Drunk me didn't feel like *me* to him.

Sex while tipsy can feel effervescent. But sex with the kind of drunk I like to get feels more like a buffer, like peering in on my life through a grease-smeared window, judging what's happening to me from a distance. In these moments, I feel as serene as a movie astronaut, suited up and floating in the endless silence of space. But it's hard to explain to someone who loves you why you prefer intimacy at a distance.

Chapter 4

A PLACE WHERE ALL THINGS ARE POSSIBLE

Halloween passed and in came November. On Election Day, I got up early to vote before work. I dressed. Did my hair, my makeup. And then hoisted a half-asleep Tyler out of bed so I could snap our photo with one of those compact, point-and-shoot Canon cameras everybody had back then. Arm out, odd angle. Flash on. Me grinning, him eyes closed and groggy. I didn't want to forget what it felt like to vote for the man who I was certain was destined to become our nation's first Black president. And I wanted to share that moment with Tyler, even though I was less sure about what destiny held for us.

By my twenties, I already doubted that America was the rise-above-its-differences country Obama claimed it to be. The first election I'd followed was 2000's "hanging chads." The Florida recount.

In 2004, I was on desk duty as an RA in my college dorm, eyes focused the entire time on the TV suspended near the ceiling, watching the count come in. It was the first presidential election I'd been old enough to vote in. John Kerry didn't thrill me. He was the Cheerios of presidential candidates—bland but good for you. Supposedly. A Democrat in office to keep your cholesterol low. Still, despite his middling appeal, I was disappointed when Kerry lost.

Dubya was not a good president. Kanye West confirmed as much less than a year into the president's second administration when he announced during an MTV telethon for Hurricane Katrina relief, "George Bush doesn't care about Black people"—not that Kanye's opinion would be worth much of anything in the years to come. Democracy had never felt fair or just—why would it? I'm a Black woman in America. But Obama felt different, like more was possible. Like we believed we actually could make a change when we chanted, *Yes, we can!*

In the brightening November sunlight, Tyler dressed, and then we walked the few blocks to the neighborhood elementary school to vote. There was already a line forming as we approached. I was the only Black person, the only person of color at all, and the only person visibly excited about what I was there to do that morning. I gave big smiles and small waves to neighbors whose faces I recognized but whose names I had not yet memorized, would never memorize. In a few more weeks, they would no longer be my neighbors.

After we voted, Tyler headed back to bed, and I went to work. The fifty-year-old eccentric millionaire didn't come to the office until after noon. He told me he liked to lie in bed until 10:00 a.m. "brainstorming," which I figured was middle-aged white-guy lingo for "wake and baking." I usually had our single-room, shoebox-size office to myself in the mornings. But that day, shortly after I arrived, Kirk stumbled in with the kinetics of Kramer from *Seinfeld*, griping about how I needed to clean up the mess that was the election. Then he looked at me and shivered slightly, as if it'd just occurred to him that I was a twentysomething Black woman, or he was finally noticing the cloud of Obama euphoria hovering over me. I was a millennial who had the audacity of hope, and Kirk was a baby boomer who did not. He sat down at his desk, opened his laptop, and didn't mention the election again.

That night, during his acceptance speech, on a stage in Chicago, beneath a veil of snowflakes, Obama said to the crowd, "If there is anyone out there who still doubts that America is a place where all things are possible . . . tonight is your answer."

Was it possible for me to stay in California? I couldn't go back to Louisville, where the memories of Tyler and me would be everywhere. They would confront me in the Kroger parking lot, triggered by the jangling sound of the grocery carts that he had pushed in high school. I would taste the absence of him on my tongue in the tap water, feel it on my skin like a humid Kentucky summer. Returning home alone would feel like flunking out of adulthood—again. First Cincinnati, now Orange County.

I decided the right answer was to stay, as if to prove to some unseen audience of my life what was possible for me.

I made calls to my family. My granny told me through my sniffles, "Didn't you get to live up in them white people's house rent-free for months? Sound like a come-up to me." A come-up, sure, but I was still broke. Fortunately, broke with a storage unit in Louisville filled with pretty decent furniture. My middle sister and her friend cracked it open, sold what could be sold, and sent me the cash for my move-out fund.

The weekend I began apartment hunting, Tyler made eggs in a basket and placed the toasted centers from the slices of bread on my plate, including his—a peace offering. He knew they were my favorite. He sat at the table while I stood by the sink and called about a room I was interested in seeing. He listened and waited for me to get off the phone. I scribbled some notes on a pad of paper, making an exaggerated show of moving forward without him.

"Want me to come with you?" he asked. In the days since he'd told me I couldn't stay, every word he spoke to me sounded like a calculated risk. He could never be sure if he'd be met with kindness or cruelty. I could tell he was concerned. I didn't do things like go to see apartments alone. I didn't even pump my own gas. It wasn't just gas station creepers. Unwanted male attention was an incessant presence in my life, but sometimes being on Tyler's arm was enough to ward off wayward men. Boyfriend as scarecrow. Still, I refused to let him chaperone my apartment hunt.

The first place I went to was listed for $700 and described as being in Huntington Beach with a view of the ocean. What the listing did not say was that it was a double-wide trailer occupied by a man, his girlfriend, her toddler, their three chocolate labs, and the various accompanying odors. I learned not to trust listings without photos. I'd initially knocked at the wrong home. Through the screen door, I watched a man rise from dinner with his family and approach me. When I asked if he was Mike, his eyes scrolled me from head to toe, and then he said, "No, but I wish I was."

I survived.

I went to see a room in a four-bedroom apartment. During the interview, when the three guys who lived there asked me why I was moving, I sat on their peanut-butter-brown leatherette couch and cried. In response, one of them asked, "You have a rice cooker, right? You mentioned that in your email." After I confirmed that, yes, I had a rice cooker, they rented me the room. This was a time before *New Girl*, and my boys didn't want to be involved in any hijinks. They had girlfriends who came around regularly (and who kept the place spotless). I had my own bathroom and off-street parking. For what I could afford, it was the best I could've hoped for.

My mother was appalled. "Lock your door at night," she said.

I tried to ease her fears. "I wouldn't move in with boys who might burst into my room while I'm sleeping, Mommy."

When Tyler offered to help move my things to my new room, again, I refused. I blatantly ignored him as he stood around watching me, unsure of what to do. A couple of months earlier, for our six-year anniversary, Tyler had bought me a pink beach cruiser. The bike took up my entire car, so I saved it for last. I went back for it when I knew he'd be home. In the garage, I saw that he'd left a letter on my bike seat. He was sorry. He loved me. He didn't want to lose me. He didn't know how to be enough for me.

It was clear that he knew I'd come to break up with him. I went inside. He'd locked himself in a bathroom. I could hear the shower running, water rolling over flesh I'd once placed my lips against—the curve of his shoulders, the base of his neck, the jut of his hip bone. Under the sound of the water, I could hear him sobbing. He was using the watermelon bodywash I'd forgotten on the windowsill; its fragrance rode the steam escaping beneath the bathroom door.

I don't remember the day I started to like-like Tyler. In high school, it takes so little to spark a crush—a stray smile, a lingering hug, and then one day, an innocent kind of desire wells up inside you and rests on your lips unspoken, like a birthday wish. Before Tyler, there'd been that boy from around the corner, the one who'd done things that it'd taken me years to speak about. To experience that just as I'd had my first taste for lust and desire was like burning my tongue on the first bite. So, every boy, like every bite after, brought discomfort that reminded me of the first one. And Tyler was safe and steady. He was the nice boy I'd needed at sixteen, but was he who I needed at twenty-three? Thirty-three? Forever? Could I stay by his side—albeit from another apartment—and endure whatever his dance dreams demanded of us? He deserved at least that much for the patient, kind love he'd blessed me with year after year, for allowing me to lean into him as a safe harbor. But I couldn't move beyond anger to compassion for the choice he'd made without me. Did that make me selfish?

He'd waited too long to tell me I needed to move. But I hadn't ever made it easy for Tyler to tell me hard things. I'd come up in a family where relationships were power struggles. I knew if I got upset enough, Tyler would give in. And if he didn't, I'd escalate. We'd parted and reconciled many times during our six years together. Maybe Tyler had finally found something he didn't want to give in on—no matter the stakes.

So, he did what he could to delay the arguments about dance school, how little he was working, and staying at his grandparents' for as long as possible. And although this was the first time our dynamic had created a housing crisis for me, this avoidance was not a new issue. And now he'd locked himself in a bathroom to avoid breaking up. Tyler wanted me to stay with him. To accept that for the time being, our love could not be at the heart of his life. To understand what this opportunity meant to him. To forgive him. Did that make him selfish?

Tyler didn't know how to tell me, I didn't know how to listen, and we didn't know how to have difficult conversations. Over the years, we'd found new ways to argue over old things. The things we argued over—Tyler's forgetfulness, his lack of initiative, and his faulty communication skills (and the things we should have argued over but never did, like my impatience, arrogance, and tendency to be domineering)—had become well worn by the time we'd arrived in Southern California. We'd brought those same problems with us from Kentucky and Ohio. And yet, we'd never learned how to solve a single one. I didn't want to still be arguing about these things in another decade with a back seat full of kids—yet another thing we disagreed on: he wanted them before thirty, and I wasn't sure I wanted them at all. I could not use disparaging looks and cold shoulders to mold the boy I loved into the man I wanted. He could not lock himself in bathrooms to avoid what was happening between us any longer: we were growing up and growing apart. Like vines roped around opposing halves of a trellis.

Maybe we were both selfish. Maybe that was OK, even if it hurt. What do two young twentysomethings actually owe each other? How can you become who you want to be when there's someone relying on you to be the person they need you to be? I was too hurt to ask myself these questions. And I was so invested in the vision of our lives that I'd held framed in my heart for six years that I couldn't even acknowledge that most people do not grow up and marry their high school sweethearts. And this fact, somehow, manages not to be a defining realization in the arc of their lives. Most people.

I'm not one of those people who's dismissive of young people's emotions. As if the only puppy-love outcome is to put it down once it gets old and starts pissing on the rug. Those early feelings may have been big and overblown, but they were real, and the joy and the pain that they brought were big and singular and honest, too. There was no choice but to live them as such.

My younger self contemplated standing on the other side of that locked bathroom door until Tyler ran out of hot water, until he was forced to come out. I thought about screaming over the rush of the shower, shaking the doorknob until the lock surrendered. But I did neither. I'd come to end our relationship, but there I was, hesitating. I loved him. But I knew I couldn't forgive him. I took a step back, out of the warmth of the steam and into the coolness of the hallway. I looked down the length of the house toward the door to the garage, open, waiting for me. I looked back at the shut, locked bathroom door. I was tired of fighting. I left.

In the driveway, I wheeled the beach cruiser over to my Jetta. I'd folded down the back seat earlier so I could cram my bike into the car. I wrestled the wide handlebars into the exact right angle that allowed me to shut the trunk. Then, I got into the car and drove, without needing the printed guidance of MapQuest, toward my new apartment, into my new life.

The prim lawns of that neighborhood by the golf course led me onto wide, well-maintained streets that guided me past large outdoor shopping plazas and onto a ramp for the 5, headed north, in the direction of a community situated between where a highway ended and the beach began.

This was Costa Mesa.

In less than two months, 2008 would be over. Ready or not—2009. I'd turn twenty-four in January, and Obama would begin his first term as president of the United States. And Tyler and I would be officially over. The arc of history and my personal narrative were overlapping and bending together toward change. Hope had delivered. Kinda.

As a nation, we'd witnessed what was possible—America could have a Black president. What else could we have? And personally, I'd discovered I could move across the country, break up with the boy I loved, and go in my own direction. What else could I do? Over the next eight years, our country would push for more and begin thinking and talking about everything differently—race, class, consent, gender, and sexuality. And I would date and drink and dance while living through these changes in small and large ways, looping back and forth between the political and the personal like a string game. Cat's cradle. Jacob's ladder. Minda's future.

PART II: CHANGE

Chapter 5

THE NOTORIOUS B.I.G. BIOPIC HAS A 52 PERCENT RATING ON ROTTENTOMATOES.COM

I knew some girls who knew some guys who'd bought some bottles, and that's how I'd found myself in a stranger's VIP section at Sutra. It was January and the night of my twenty-fourth birthday party. I was tipsy on arrival, but that didn't stop anyone at the club from pouring me glasses of Grey Goose. Girls love Grey Goose. For every sip of vodka I drank, I sloshed five on the floor. Some poor guy had probably paid a dollar for each drop. Bottles went for $300 at Sutra. Men bought them—and it was almost always men—because a place to rest and free booze lured in women, calves burning, feet sore in high heels.

I sat in VIP, quietly watching the flashing lights like a baby watches a mobile, and let the loud music drown out my thoughts. I was super drunk as a necessary distraction from my incoming quarter-life crisis. I didn't know who I was if I wasn't a girlfriend. I'd spent all my young-adult years thus far as one. The care and maintenance of a relationship had been a shield against self-introspection. Unhappy? Frustrated? Disappointed? There was a boyfriend to blame for that. There were arguments to be had. There was drama to dredge up. Not sure what I wanted to do with my life? No worries—I could focus my energy on what *he* should be doing with *his* life to improve *our* life. While I was with Tyler, it felt normal, even so young, or maybe because we were so young, for a relationship to be all-consuming. My friends back home in Kentucky were in similar situations. We went to school. We went to work. We had ambitions. Sure. But our social lives, our emotional well-being, and our dreams for the future hinged on our dating status.

Following the breakup, my future was a question mark. My heart was off-kilter. And my social life rerouted. I'd become a woman struck by indecision, standing in the grocery store, holding the freezer door open long enough to give me frostbite. Loading up on blueberry muffins. Blueberry Eggo mini waffles. And those absurd Jimmy Dean pancake-wrapped sausages on a stick—also blueberry. I didn't even like blueberry. My ex liked blueberry. Aisle after aisle, I put groceries in and pulled groceries out of my cart, trying to find my own appetite.

I was no longer a girlfriend. And I was no longer a sister, a daughter, or a best friend. At least, not in the same way. I was newly single and in a new city. I'd also lost my location-based identity: Who was I if I wasn't in Louisville, where everyone knew whose grandbaby I was? Ask yourself who you are and try to answer without referring to your family, your friends, your relationship, where you live, or what you do. My father used to be one phone call from helping me out in every scenario, from loaning me his hi-tech laser leveler to hang photos with precision to showing up at the scene of a car accident to console me and offer counsel. My mother could no longer love me through elaborate meals, a plate of my favorites—golden, crispy bone-in pork chops; soy sauce fried chicken wings; thick slices of strawberry cake topped with huge globs of frosting—hidden in the microwave to make sure I got my share. And I wasn't around to hassle my sisters' boyfriends. I went from taking photos during a Friday night out with friends to sitting on my bed, liking my friends' Facebook photos. Even in Cincinnati, I'd had my high school sweetheart as my anchor, and we were little more than an hour's drive from the people who knew and loved us. I'd only ever defined myself through those connections. Then I became a solo traveler in a strange land. A southerner in Southern California.

I couldn't see that there was also freedom in not being known. Louisville had been like living in a mirror maze. Everywhere I looked, people reflected an image of me—who they expected me to be as a partner, as a daughter, as a friend. I wish I could have seen that Southern California was providing me with the space to change and evolve unhindered. I wish I had used that time to figure myself out. Instead, I made quick friends and I partied. A lot.

After I was at the club for a while, a boy in a white tee with a deep V-neck sat down beside me in VIP. He had lines of ink tattooed beneath the two halves of his collarbone, but I couldn't read the words in the millisecond-long strobes of light that chopped through the darkness.

"It's my birthday!" I drunk babbled at him.

"I want to dance with the birthday girl," he said.

He guided me around the velvet rope and into the crush of commoners on the dance floor. The strobe light made it feel like we were moving in flash frames. I was so drunk by that point, I was basically just leaning on him, trying to stay upright in heels. We didn't "dance" long.

Seated back in VIP, he took my phone. "What should I save myself under, so you remember who I am?" As a birthday gift, my father had upgraded me to my first iPhone, and this dude would be the first new number in it.

"Tatts—Best Dancer Ever."

He laughed. "I don't think that's true, but OK."

"I have to tell you something, though."

"OK," he said, leaning in.

For the occasion, one of the beauty-counter girls I used to work with had done my makeup. A shock of hot-pink lipstick and my first pair of false lashes. I took an eyelash between two fingers and slowly peeled it from my lid. Then I peeled off the other and placed both, like twin black caterpillars, in the palm of his hand. "These aren't my real lashes."

Another former coworker, sitting on the other side of us, who was far more sober than me, saw the horror on his face and snatched the lashes from his hand, shoving them in my purse.

"It's OK; it doesn't hurt at all! I promise," she assured him, patting his shoulder.

I smiled and closed my eyes.

The next morning, I lay in bed alone and thought about how it'd been a little petty of Drunk Minda to save that boy in my phone under "BEST DANCER EVER" when my ex was training to become a professional dancer. I traced the flower pattern on my duvet cover with my fingers and thought about what might come next. Sunlight as gray as dishwater washed over me.

Tatts and I made movie plans. I was going on my first adult first date. I felt giddy and nervous and alive, like a colt on wobbly legs in a green, green pasture, fresh to the world. I knew hardly anything about this man; we had less than an hour's worth of history together. There was nothing for me to silently seethe over. Conjuring new love was light work in comparison to resuscitating an old one. I didn't really have any expectations for Tatts; otherwise, I might have bothered to ask my friends about him or had a few phone conversations with him, anything that would have served as a warning. But I was fresh. And new. And naive. The only thing that mattered to me about Tatts was that he was not my ex. He was a teething ring, baby steps back into dating.

I was so nervous when we met up; I don't remember if we hugged when we first saw each other or anything we talked about before the movie. V-necks must have been his thing because he was wearing another one. He bought two tickets for *Notorious*, the Biggie Smalls biopic that was so poorly shot, it looked like it was a joint production between Lifetime and BET. Seated beside Tatts in the dark, my body pulsed with anticipation. I was unsure how dating as an adult would differ from dating as a teenager. Would he make a move? Would he try to hold my hand? Would he put his arm around me? Were these things that adults did on movie dates? Were these things that adult women wanted adult men to do on movie dates?

He tentatively placed a hand on my knee. Then he started rubbing my leg. Like really working up some friction. Was he trying to jack off my kneecap? I didn't stop him. He'd paid for the movie tickets; it seemed fair to let him rub a hole in my ten-dollar tights if that's what he really wanted to do. For ninety minutes straight, he rubbed. Biggie fucked Lil' Kim. He married Faith Evans. He beefed with Tupac. He died. Puff Daddy danced in the background through it all. And Tatts continued to rub.

"Did you like the movie?" he asked me as we walked out into the lobby. He slung a tattooed arm across my shoulder.

"Yeeeeah," I lied. The Notorious B.I.G. biopic has a 52 percent rating on RottenTomatoes.com. It deserves less. I snuck a look at my tights in the light to see if his rubbing had created a shiny patch on my knee.

The next day at work, I got a text from Tatts. He wanted to make it clear that he was not interested in a "wifey." I wasn't trying to be Tatt's wifey; my tights couldn't endure that many evenings with him. All I wanted to do was think of someone other than Tyler. To no longer be plagued by those thoughts that snuck up on me during the peaceful rhythm of simple tasks. Staple, staple. *Does he still love me?* Chew, chew. *Do I love him?* Pour, pour. *Did I make a mistake?* Brush, brush. *Was he the mistake?*

At the end of our date, Tatts had kissed me real quick, then looked surprised the kiss had happened, even though he'd initiated it. It wasn't the big, dramatic, romantic moment I'd wanted for the end of my first adult first date, but it was a kiss.

I was one more step removed from returning to my ex. There seemed to be unspoken rules around this from our previous break-ups: Flirting with someone else is mild, and the jealousy from that can bring a little heat to the reunion. Coming back from a kiss is iffy but doable—I know because I'd done it a couple of times. And attempting to reunite after one of us had slept with someone else, well, that'd be nearly impossible. I was Tyler's first, and I couldn't see him looking past me sleeping with another dude when he'd only ever slept with me. It would be a decisive end to our on-again, off-again love affair.

Tatts served a purpose. But that was all. Over text, he also shared that he thought it was weird I worked in an office. I didn't know what he found so weird about office work. Maybe he'd only dated retail girls. Or did he think it was weird that I specifically worked in an office? Maybe he didn't expect drunk chicks who peeled off their eyelashes in nightclubs to work a nine-to-five. Tatts worked in a department store on the Visuals team. Basically, he dressed mannequins for a living. This, apparently, was not considered a weird form of employment.

A few days later, Tatts texted me again. He'd decided to look past my "bizarre" occupation: "Maybe we could just mess around?"

"Yeah, OK," I told him. I wanted to experience the hookup culture my generation was supposedly known for.

"Cool, can't wait to show you my Louisville Slugger," he replied.

There was one issue: he still lived with his ex. Just until their lease was up, he'd said. But that didn't explain why he couldn't come to my place. Every time we made plans, he flaked. In retrospect, he was probably lying, presenting a current girlfriend as a past-tense situation. But I didn't see that at the time.

We never did hook up. At one point, he asked me to send him a naked pic—"It doesn't have to include your face"—and I was so offended that we stopped texting. It was a time before Kim Kardashian had fully built an empire off a sex tape.

Tatts had proven to be a terrible distraction. I wondered what Tyler was up to. I was ready to return to the graveyard of failed romances and dig our relationship back up with my bare hands. I was still angry. I still felt betrayed. I doubt I'd grown any more receptive to listening to things I didn't want to hear. I was just hurt and lonely, and in the past, getting back together had been the easiest means to not feel either of those emotions any longer—at least for a little while, until I'd grow restless and dissatisfied again and restart the cycle. We'd never actually stayed broken up long enough for me to discover what was on the other side of heartbreak.

Chapter 6

A Grate Night

In February, I spent thirty minutes standing in the greeting-card aisle at Target. I wanted to get a card in the mail to arrive by Tyler's birthday. I imagined that if I chose the right card, one with words that read flowery and suggested, "Maybe I made a mistake—happy birthday," he would show up on my doorstep by Valentine's Day with flowers and renewed pleas for reconciliation. But less than a month into our breakup, before I could even send the card, it became clear that my little fantasy was not our future.

Tyler had a *grate* night and a wonderful morning.

I was at work in Laguna Beach when I saw it. I'd suffered through two whole hours of Excel sheets and self-restraint before logging on to Facebook to pull up his page. I should have unfriended him, but I didn't know how to let him go. How could I shift from knowing everything to knowing nothing at all? There's no social-interaction transition plan in a breakup. There was just complete and total *ex*-communication or what I was doing—pretending I had it together enough to stay connected.

I checked his page constantly for any sign that he missed me. Generally, there was very little for me to snoop through online. The posts on his wall were mostly his ridic friends posting ridic YouTube videos ("dude look! this guy used his buddy's ass crack to launch a bottle rocket LOL!!!!!"). Maintaining a Facebook friendship with him did have the added benefit of exposing him to my carefully curated independent-woman posts: "I just changed my own brake light! Who needs a boyfriend anyways? :)." I alternated those posts with lyrics from the emo-as-hell Dashboard Confessional songs we'd listened to together in high school.

Subtext: I was doing just fine without him, but I would be willing to take him back if he'd ask.

But he wasn't going to ask.

Tyler had a grate night and a wonderful morning.

I sat at my desk and glared at that sentence. I leaned toward my monitor, as if a closer look was going to force the words of his status update to reveal more than they already had. I double-clicked his name, and a chat window bloomed on the screen. "It's 'great,'" I typed.

"Oh thanks," he responded and fixed his status update.

I wasn't sure why he thought I was just leaping into his messages to offer spelling tips.

"Are you seeing someone else?"

"Yes."

I punched my fingers down on each key at full force. "And then you posted it all over Facebook for all of our friends to see?!"

Despite our being broken up, in those early days of social media, twenty-four-year-old Minda felt entitled to a certain level of decorum—that meant your ex was not allowed to quickly move on in plain view of your mutual contacts.

A few sweeps of my mouse and one click later, and I'd done angrily what I should have done sensibly in the first place—unfriend.

My phone rumbled over and over on the desk next to me. I leaned back in my chair and waited for Tyler to get his fill of being sent to voice mail so that I could blast out a mass distress text to my three best friends and my middle sister back home. The iPhone made it possible to text the entire saga in a way the T9 keypad on my flip phone would not have allowed.

It was as if my friends and sister had huddled up before replying; their responses were an identical chorus: "That asshole!"

"Hey, Minda." A familiar voice drifted into the office.

My head snapped up from my phone. "Kirk."

My boss stood in the doorway in his usual designer denim and the dune-colored boots I'd watched him order online the month before. He'd spent more on them than what he paid me every two weeks. There was always an air of tension between us when Kirk arrived at the office, as if he'd caught me in the middle of doing something—or more accurately, in the middle of doing nothing. He had never been very clear about my job responsibilities, so there wasn't much for me to do most days. I earned my keep by getting up at 1:00 a.m. to make sure Kinko's was printing our posters properly, or by magically finding the one store selling pinwheels in the entire county when a client forgot to order them for a shoot, or by sitting close to Kirk and being completely still while he worked because he needed my "energy."

A man in a white short-sleeved dress shirt who was only as tall as Kirk's shoulder stood beside him. The Apple specialist. But our appointment with him wasn't until 4:00 p.m. I looked at the clock in the corner of my computer screen: 4:00 p.m. Out the window, the gold-plated sky from the start of the day had deepened into copper. The morning was long gone.

I forced a smile. Kirk threw his worn leather satchel onto his wooden desk, sat down, and slid out his laptop—the recently launched

MacBook Air (he really could have afforded to pay me more). The specialist took a seat in the chair across from him.

"Stu and I talked about my problems on the way up. Shouldn't take long to work out. He can get started on yours first," Kirk said.

Speak. I couldn't. It was like my jaw was joined to my tear ducts, like opening my mouth would lower the dam, too. I was too overwhelmed to remain professional. Kirk and Stu waited. Stu stood up, moved closer, tapped the top of my iMac, and asked, "So, what's the matter?"

"I-I-I just found out my ex is fucking some other chick, and-and-and it's on Facebook." The cascade burst forth. I shuttered my face with my hands.

I'd only once mentioned my breakup to Kirk. I'd returned from an errand, and he'd taken in the way my jeans slouched off one hip. He'd told me I looked "good." He'd said it more like someone assessing the paint job on a new car than a man leering at his employee half his age. Even as I sat at my desk, I felt the exaggerated gap between my waist and my pants, excess fabric raised in static ripples in my lap.

Kirk spoke up first. "Well, that's a boat rocker."

I lowered my hands and nodded. My boat had certainly been rocked.

Then Stu spoke. "Don't worry about that boy. You're so pretty. There'll be tons of boys. If I were just a little bit younge—"

"Um," Kirk interrupted. He then said to me, "Why don't you grab a Coke downstairs? We can make do here for a few without you." In that moment, Kirk was kind, but by the end of the summer, he would fire me—I assume for sending him an email outlining his escalating anger issues.

I rushed to the stairwell, down the steps, and out onto the sidewalk. Our office was on the Pacific Coast Highway, across the street from a row of shops that backed up against stairs leading down to the beach. They called our building the Cruise Ship because restaurants offering various cuisines served up meals on every floor. Cumin, garlic, and pepper mixed with the saltwater air that blew in off the ocean, and I inhaled all the smells by the gasping, heaving lungful. I clutched a parking meter, doubled over the curb, arm across what was once my belly, and dry heaved into the street.

My ex was fucking someone else.

My friend Chandra called. As I told her everything, I crossed the street, wandered past the shops, and stepped out onto an overlook. The ocean rushed in, greedy for the taste of the shore, and the copper sky became streaked with tendrils of magenta that darkened and broadened into wide streams of sangria. After Chandra, I spoke with Stephanie, then Tabitha, and lastly, my middle sister, Jasmine.

Beachgoers rolled up their towels. Soon it would be just the surf and the shore murmuring secrets to one another. I walked back to my office building and sat on a bench out front, then dialed one of the few numbers I still knew by heart.

"I have to go to work soon," Tyler said as a greeting. I imagined him standing in his grandparents' kitchen. I could see him staring out the window at the pool and the hummingbird feeder. He'd insisted we drip red dye into the sugar-and-water mixture, although I'd assured him the birds would come even without the food coloring.

"I want to know who she is." I watched the shop owners across the street lock their doors, flip their signs from "OPEN" to "CLOSED." The PCH was choked with traffic. Everything was moving on around me. I alone remained still.

"You don't want to know that. You broke up with me."

But I did want to know. Throughout our relationship, I'd worried that Tyler couldn't really know if he wanted to spend a lifetime with me when he'd had such limited experiences with other girls. What if he didn't actually love me, and our relationship was more of a sentimental, emotional attachment? I found that I'd gone straight from that concern to ascribing an incredible amount of meaning to him sleeping with someone new. I'd been down to have sex with Tatts with no interest in a relationship, but then I'd gotten bleary-eyed at work because my ex had moved on first. I wasn't being fair.

Again, although I had no right, I demanded to know who she was. Finally, he told me. She was a girl from his dance classes. They'd started dating only a few days after we'd broken up. "Were you two—" I gripped the edge of the bench; the splintered wood pricked my palm. Had he cheated?

"Never. If you hadn't left me, it would have never happened." His voice sounded weepy. He was hurting, too. My hand relaxed. I believed him. I thought back to the day I picked up my bike and he was sobbing in the shower. Our actions and our emotions can be out of sync. I'd lost enough weight to need a new wardrobe while also flirting with Tatts. I'd already answered the nine hundred questions necessary to set up an OkCupid profile. That didn't mean I wasn't crying myself to sleep every night. Somehow, knowing he was still sad took some of the sting out of him moving on so soon. But I didn't tell him that.

"I can't get into all of this. I need to go back to work," I said instead. "Goodbye." Kirk and Stu were waiting. Enough time had passed for me to drink an entire case of Coke. Soon, Laguna Beach would be blanketed in navy.

I may have initiated the breakup, but Tyler had done what neither one of us had ever been able to do before—he'd made it final. I had to let go. We were at an age, at a place in our lives, and in a portion of the country where our relationship no longer made sense. I was looking for a heartbreak cure, but backtracking through a heart I'd already broken wasn't where I'd find it. I couldn't go back to an ex and find happiness any more than I could go back to the person I'd once been who'd been satisfied with that life. I was fresh. And new. And naive.

Chapter 7

When Henry Met Minda

When I was growing up, the mall closest to my home had these elaborate fountains. They were carpeted over at some point when they became too expensive to maintain. But in the '90s, my mom used to pass out pennies and tell us kids to make a wish.

Some kids wish for their Christmas list.

Some kids wish for world peace.

I wished for it to be Valentine's Day. Every. Single. Day. Pink skies, heart-shaped clouds—like Groundhog Day, but make it romantic. I fantasized about living in that serene, happily-ever-after moment when the girl and the guy in the movie have found their way back to each other, and it's going to be all right.

Love stories were my favorite plot. In elementary school, I'd read an entire case of romance novels by playing Harlequin on their own pay-a-dollar ploy. It was basically the book equivalent of a CD-of-the-month club. My dad helped me craft the letter informing them that I was underage; therefore, their monthly subscription contract was non-binding. My father had been far more concerned with sticking it to the man than he was with monitoring my reading.

The books followed the same formula: woman meets man she can't stand. Turns out, that tension is actually sexual tension. Woman is humbled in some way, followed by sex (women must always be humbled in exchange for our sexual gratification). Then there's some conflict, and they fall out. Next, they figure out they can't go on without their heart's desire. Finally, they find their way back to each other. That's the important part. That's how love keeps us safe, secure, and happy—if we just remember to follow the formula.

I was a kid who dreamed of meeting a man and making it work. Maybe I found comfort in love stories because they held the secret to what was missing from my parents' marriage. Their relationship was like a fallout-scene supercut from the books and movies I found myself obsessed with. They just never made it to the part of the formula where they found their way back to each other. And when I was twelve, they stopped trying altogether.

Their divorce was for the best. But it still left me distraught, and my entire existence was disrupted. Witnessing the end of my parents' marriage deepened my subconscious belief that if I wanted happiness, if I wanted stability, if I wanted more than misery in the morning and arguing in the evening, then I needed to live my life by the rules of a love story.

And this was the belief I loved by while dating my high school sweetheart. If there weren't flowers on Valentine's Day, there were tears. I demanded a promise ring, even when I had no so-called purity to promise Tyler. Our breakup meant I was flung backward in my love-story plot. I'd never felt further from happily ever after. Maybe, by my twenties, I should have outgrown the Disney-style love stories girls are indoctrinated into. It wasn't like I'd never heard that kind of romance was unrealistic. But when you're a Black girl and denied depictions of love—either by movies that cast us as the two-dimensional, sassy assistant or skewed facts that market us as the least desirable demographic—do you believe the lie that says you can find your great love if

The Heartbreak Years

you attempt to follow an impossible formula, or the one that tells you you're inherently unworthy? Someday, I'd learn there is a thing called "nuance" and that the truth lives someplace between "either" and "or," but still young and newly single, I clung to the only plot I knew, even if it was flawed. Even if it demanded that my safety and self-esteem be subject to the whims of men.

After meeting Tatts, there'd been other men—I'd even slept with one or two—but none of them were viable relationship options. Of course, I rarely knew this going into a new situation. The meet-cute is a faulty indicator of compatibility. I'd mistakenly believed that the more adorable your initial encounter with a man, the more likely your everlasting love. The spark was a sign that this time was different. The dude yelling crude things at you from his car? Not meant to be. How you met a man had to be the kind of story that made your friends lean in a little closer. It needed that dash of magic to separate it from the everyday. It had to be a moment your mind could return to when things got rough, a moment that made you still believe. An ordinary love doesn't last for decades or beat the odds against divorce, I seemed to think. The meet-cute was a must.

The night I met Henry was like the beginning of my long-awaited meet-cute-turned-happily-ever-after story. I was at Sharkeez, the one on the Newport Beach peninsula. Sharkeez's mascot is a shark with a gold tooth, wearing a sombrero, strumming a three-stringed guitar. At the time, the place marketed itself as a "Mesquite Mex Broiler," but what Sharkeez was really known for was its early-night three-for-one drinks special. A Sharkeez night was the type of night you let someone else take responsibility for getting you home safely—in retrospect, a reckless choice at a bar where a bouncer once hauled me out for getting loud with a man who'd grabbed my ass beneath my dress as I'd shimmied past.

That night at the bar, the floor was sticky, the air was sticky, my armpits were sticky. Boys ricocheted from girl to girl like pinballs

45

zinging around an arcade game. The one standing in front of me was plugging my number into his outdated Palm Pilot. "M-I- . . . M . . . No, *M* not *L*. M-I-N-D . . . *D*, not *B*. D . . . A," I said, spelling out the letters to my name, starting and stopping again as he strained to hear me over the music. He was Nigerian, but when I heard his accent, I'd assumed he was British. He wasn't the typical Sharkeez bro in a graphic tee and jeans. He wore a pressed button-down, unbuttoned just so, and expensive jeans, notably without a Von Dutch patch stitched across the butt. Despite his relative classiness, he was boring me. He'd approached me with that coy, hands-in-pocket kind of shuffle that works well for dudes in rom-coms who accidentally run into you while you're rushing out of a coffee shop. But that energy came across as nervous and unconfident against the hectic backdrop of the latest Lil' Wayne remix and servers in crop tops shilling buckets of oversize plastic syringes filled with blue Jell-O—a shot *and* a pun. After Henry gave me his name, I didn't even bother saving his number in my phone.

A caravan of my girls rolled by on their way to the restroom, towing me along with them. In the long-ass line, my new friends gabbed. The one behind me said over my shoulder, "You've been holding up so well. We all just keep waiting for you to break down so we can be there for you. But you seem so OK with everything."

Everything that had happened with my ex left me looking like a week-old manicure. I was polished and shiny, but if you looked closely, you could see me wearing down around the edges. I didn't want my hurt to chip away at any more of me or to reveal that I was still in pain. I was scared to be an emotional burden for people I'd only known for a few months.

The line moved forward, and we crossed the threshold into the restroom. The stank of girl piss and fresh puke mashed us in the face. There was a woman standing in front of the sinks, her chest and shoulders stuttering up and down fast, staccato-like. She was inconsolable.

"What happened?" someone asked.

Her friend rubbed the small of her back. "Her boyfriend of four years just dumped her."

Seeing someone else publicly grieve a similar loss—just as too many rounds of three-for-one rum and pineapple juices hit my system—was too much. "My boyfriend of six and a half years is sleeping with someone new!" I wailed. The girl and I crumpled into each other.

Heartbreak Hotel: occupancy, two.

Girls squeezed around us to pump soap into their palms and rinse their hands in the sink. Someone stretched an arm across us to tug on the lever of the forever-empty paper towel dispenser. Eventually, one of my friends extracted me from the sobbing stranger. "Let's go outside and get you some fresh air," she advised.

Afterward, we went back inside and I sat on a bench off the dance floor, dabbing at the corner of my eyes with a wadded-up napkin, my runny black mascara turning it gray. The boy from earlier, with the accent, cut through the crowd and said into my ear, "Don't cry. Just dance."

Henry stepped back and reached his hand out. I threw down my wet napkin and placed my hand in his. It was as if I floated to him. I didn't even feel my $1.99 flip-flops stick-unstick to the floor. Meet-cute standard: met.

We tried to talk over the music as we danced. Frustrated he couldn't hear my thoughts on gritty-British-rapper-turned-American-loved-songstress Estelle, he led me outside. He walked me to the side of the building that faced a parking lot and the main road. Cars drove up and down the strip, their drivers looking for a good time along the stretch of shoreside bars. Close by, the ocean rocked itself to sleep, salt on its breath. The peninsula was well lit. I could hear the music bumping inside the bar, now muffled, and the sound of people leaving and entering through Sharkeez's front door. I was all hopped up on cheap rum and even cheaper ideas of romance courtesy of my childhood infatuation with Harlequin novels. Dashing stranger was a fantasy I was down for.

Alcohol's ability to numb concerns makes it possible for young women to brave the threat of sexual assault for the promise of romance while simultaneously leaving us defenseless against prospective violence. I didn't street race or skydive or wrestle bears, but I did stand in semi-dark places alone with men—while drunk.

I leaned back against the side of the building; the rough bricks scratched my bare shoulders. We continued to talk about music, and with each artist that came up, Henry leaned in a little closer to me. His cologne overpowered. Van Cleef & Arpels, a luxury brand I'd never heard of.

Henry kissed me while I was midsentence—a classic rom-com move. Before the kiss grew even a single degree in intensity, he stopped. It felt almost innocent in nature, even though I was drunk, on the side of a bar, and knew nearly nothing about the man with his mouth on mine. Small details.

His phone buzzed; his friends were leaving. We walked around front. It was last call; people tumbled out like Yahtzee dice. My friends soon flanked me, and Henry walked over to his, already in their car, engine running, headlights gleaming. He rolled the back window down and waved goodbye to me as the car pulled off.

"Don't forget to call me!" I cried out.

"I won't," he shouted back, his words fading into the night.

A rando drunk dude passing me muttered, "He's not going to call."

"Yes, he will," I said.

He didn't.

A month later, my friend Adam visited. We pulled into West Hollywood around dusk. It was the first time for both of us. Large rainbow flags dangled from every storefront. Two men held hands. Nearby, a man casually wrapped his arm around the waist of another, rested a cheek against his shoulder. It was March 2009. Crossing into

West Hollywood was like leaping into an alternate reality, one where the state of California had not passed a same-sex marriage ban four months earlier. This superior reality would seep eastward, beyond the sidewalks of West Hollywood, and across time to find Adam nine years later in a small Indiana town just across the river from Louisville, where I would watch him clasp hands with the man he loved and—with the blessing of their friends, family, and the law—vow their lives to each other.

At our second-to-last bar of the night, the go-go dancers wore too-tiny shorts that turned their toned asses into the arched curve of a question mark. Lifeguard whistles dangled from chains around their necks. Every few minutes, a different dancer brought his whistle to his lips. Puckered. And blew. And each time, my eyes rose upward, as if in worship at the feet of a saint.

Everything smelled slick.

Under the lights of howling red sirens, dancers poured shots into the sprawled-wide mouths of the crowd. Sometimes with a hand cradled under a chin, like a bottle to a lamb—benevolent farmers nursing us to ecstasy.

Happily sandwiched between a wonder-boy duo, I only left the dance floor for more drinks for Adam and me. In my twenties, there were few feelings more flattering than being a pretty girl in a gay bar, the men adorning my D-cups with strings of compliments. Their attention came without end-of-the-night expectations. There were no straight-male egos to cautiously two-step around. There could be flirting, there could be touching, bodies against bodies, without the heightened fear of transgression.

I knew from stories my gay friends had told me that even if my personal risk was reduced by the absence of straight men, sexual harassment—and worse—could happen, and had happened to them, in these spaces. And gay bars were spaces that I wasn't entitled to.

So, I wondered why there were no overtly sexual places for straight women calibrated for our comfort. In straight bars, I had to use my sexuality to entice men, dialing the performance up or down based on my own desires or sense of danger. Is it because a woman in control is not what the majority considers a sexy woman? A self-indulgent woman is not a sexy woman. A safe woman is not a sexy woman. Women must remain approachable, even when we don't feel safe. Murderers in horror movies take out the sorority house or the cheerleaders. They never sneak up on the girls' track team.

I ordered cocktails from the bar at the center of the club. The bartender prepared the drinks, then wrung a lemon wedge out over the glasses and used two fingers to tuck the spent rind into my cleavage. Inside my clutch, my iPhone shivered to life under my arm. I peeked into my purse at the text on the screen: "Wherever you are, I hope you're smiling."

I walked our drinks over to Adam, who was standing at the base of a white pedestal, chatting with a go-go dancer. The dancer dropped into a squat to hear Adam better. He rested his forearms on his knees, his bulging red shorts now at eye level.

"Who is this?" I texted back after handing Adam his glass.

"It's Henry," came the reply.

"Henry who?"

"From Sharkeez."

Annoyed, I dropped my phone back into my bag and returned to dancing with the wonder-boy duo.

After our night ogling go-go dancers, Adam and I decided to start the next day with brunch at the Abbey, an iconic gay bar. By that afternoon, we were back in Orange County and on the beach. We lay on the sand, offering our human vessels to the sun god. I told Adam about the text. He encouraged me to at least find out what had happened. I called Henry. "Why didn't you call?"

His proper Queen's English soared up from the iPhone. "Me? Call you? Darling, I was waiting for it to go the other way around."

This was ludicrous to me in a way that almost feels absurd now—
me text someone that *I* wanted to hear from? So often with dating, I
equated initiative with desperation. I needed to feel supremely desired.
It was a time before Tiana, Moana, and Elsa. I was still asleep, waiting
to be kissed. As a '90s kid, I'd gone to dozens of Take Your Daughter
to Work Days, where I'd been told I could be whatever I wanted to be
when I grew up. But apparently, that only applied to the classroom or
the workplace. No one was telling me that if I wanted to go out with a
guy, I should just ask him. No one was saying, "Don't be coy—insist on
a label for your relationship." No, women were to be proactive in every
other aspect of our lives and passive in love. Pretty, but not know it.
Available, but not demanding of his time. Otherwise, you'd be branded
clingy and needy. But it was actually the self-imposed waiting for a
man to reveal his mind that put me in the position of uncertainty that
inspired desperate behavior.

"Fine, fine. I'm free after I take my friend to the airport tomorrow," I told him after a little verbal tug-of-war over who should have
called who.

"Sunday is God's day," Henry said. "I've got Mass."

Adam and I exchanged a look. I'd felt more holy on the dance floor
in West Hollywood than I'd ever felt sitting in a church pew.

Henry and I made plans for later in the week.

Henry lived in the shadow of the Crystal Cathedral, an all-glass
church that looked like a shard of the Emerald City plunked down
in Southern California. When the cathedral was first built, you could
stand in the chapel at the very top and see groves and groves of orange
trees. Now the view was less spectacular, shopping centers and office
buildings laid out along dark-ash-gray strips of road.

To be cautious, I'd suggested Henry and I meet out, but he didn't
have a car; he was an international grad school student. He insisted on
a ride. It was still a time before Uber. My first instinct was to say no.
Sober, it was a lot harder to forget that I didn't know this guy. Alone

with him in my car, any number of things could go wrong. However, my fears were somewhat quelled in the days leading up to seeing him. We'd had several lengthy phone calls where he'd come off as grandfatherly. He didn't drink or smoke. He was against tattoos—"Why ruin that beautiful golden skin from God?" He didn't "believe" in strippers. To be sure, many of Henry's views were regressive even more than a decade ago, but over the phone, that posh accent of his seduced me with every syllable he spoke. Although none of those viewpoints precludes anyone from being a rapist, I'd decided I trusted him enough to let him ride shotgun.

That is, until I saw him on the other side of the security gate at his apartment complex in a pair of low-slung khakis and no shirt. His skin was the deep brown black of rich soil, his bare chest and abs as impressive as those of the West Hollywood go-go dancers I'd gazed at with Adam. Although I had an appreciation for what I was seeing, I couldn't think of any positive motives behind not pulling on a shirt before I arrived. He'd likely given little thought to his choice to pop up half-clothed, but I had been intentional about dressing conservatively for our date—a belief that attire could dissuade any assumptions he may have made about a girl who'd kissed him the same night he'd found her crying in a bar. As if barreling past a woman's boundaries was frequently born of some misunderstanding based on the length of her skirt. I'm just now realizing how much of my dating life involved this push and pull of wearing next to nothing in a crowded bar to draw a man's eyes, then arriving on a first date mainly covered up but with one exception—just cleavage, or just a short skirt, or just a little midriff—to signal that I wasn't a prude but I was to be respected. These were superficial methods of manipulating the situation when the other party was likely physically stronger than me and had the norms of our culture on his side.

The gate to Henry's complex slid open, and I drove through. Henry motioned for me to roll down my window. "Park along here. I've got to finish dressing."

"Cool. I'll wait."

"But I want you to meet my roommate."

Two men I didn't know in an apartment? It was daylight, but I was picturing a series of dark rooms. Henry must have read the fear on my face.

He smiled. "Come now, not everyone is after *'that thing, that thing,'*" he said, singing a few words from a Lauryn Hill song. I trusted that smile. I got out of the car and promised myself I wouldn't stay in his apartment for more than five minutes—as if nothing too terrible could happen in less time than that.

Nervousness lined my stomach and thickened as we walked deeper and deeper into the apartment complex. He led me over a couple of walkways and up a few different sets of stairs. There was no way I'd remember how to get back to my car.

By the time we reached his apartment, I had forgotten about his roommate, who was standing near their front door, waiting for us. I stood in the doorway so Henry could not close the door, so I would not hear the click of it locking shut behind me. Anyone passing in the hallway could look in on us. That felt safe. The same late-afternoon sunlight that was plentiful outside joined us in the apartment through the open door and many windows.

His roommate was nearly seven feet tall, with a European accent I couldn't place. He reminded me of a young, attractive version of Lurch from *The Addams Family*. Henry wasn't much taller than me, maaaaaybe 5′7″, and I could only imagine how the two of us looked, standing there together with our heads bent back, looking at his roommate like he was our own personal Gulliver. Henry left to put on a shirt in his bedroom. I wouldn't move any farther into the apartment than the doorway, like a dog that had been trained not to leave the linoleum. His roommate was also about as chatty as Lurch, and we passed the minutes in silence. Maybe he sensed that I was worried that he was going to rape me. When Henry returned from his room and we were finally off, I felt like I had survived something far braver than standing in the doorway of a boy's apartment. The boy from around the corner had taught me an early lesson in what could happen behind locked doors.

I was not always certain what was paranoia and what was self-preservation. How could I heed my heart without endangering my body? Why was acting on my wants so profoundly risky? Any amount of trust given to a man that proved to be undeserved would be publicly cast as a misstep on my part. I don't agree with that. But I'm not exempt from judgment, regardless of my choices. I couldn't just shut down my desires to prioritize remaining safe because if I listened to those fears and acted on them, I'd also be judged for my enduring singleness (not to mention, I had no interest in a lifetime of unmet wants). I was somehow expected to maneuver the inherent risk in dating but also be entirely responsible if that risk led to my physical, emotional, or mental demise.

Henry and I weren't sure what we wanted to do on our date. We ended up in Anaheim, not far from his apartment, at an open-air, multistoried mall, a capitalism jungle gym. We walked around making silly chatter. When we passed a Cheesecake Factory, Henry asked me if I was hungry.

"I could split dessert."

He led me inside and said, "I've never been here before. What flavor should we get?"

"How about the peanut butter chocolate? Or the strawberry short-cake? Or . . ." I suggested five different slices, poking my finger in the air at each one.

Henry turned to the cashier. "We'll have each of those. To go."

Used to men who acted like buying you a drink at the bar was some great act of generosity, I was impressed by his gesture. He was spending more on cheesecake than it cost me to fill up my gas tank.

We headed back into the night and spread our slices out on a plastic picnic table away from the tourist-trap restaurant. We took turns using our spoons to carve thick chunks of cheesecake for each other. We sat and ate and talked. I felt like I shared more than I heard. Henry always seemed to ask more questions than he answered. I did learn that he'd attended boarding school in London, went to Mass every Sunday, and had seven brothers and sisters. "What were your parents thinking?" I asked.

"That children are a blessing," he said, as if no one had ever felt otherwise.

We headed back to my car. As we walked up the down ramp into the parking garage, braced by concrete on all sides, he reached over and took my hand in his. Heart: flutter. With Henry, could I be more than the sad, crying girl I was at the bar?

Inside the car, Henry lugged my big black binder of five hundred CDs from the back seat and splayed it open across his lap, gliding his finger over the edge of each sheet, flipping to the next, doling out praise and criticism over my collection as he saw fit. It was a time before streaming killed the compact disc. Henry would pop a CD in and skip through a few tracks before ejecting it, returning it to its sleeve, and popping another CD in. A few years later, while packing to move to Denver, I would consider throwing out the entire binder. My baby sister—suffering a breakup from her own high school sweetheart, during which she'd lost many of her CDs—would plead with me to send it to her. So much of her tastes had been shaped by mine as I drove her around in my car, shuffling through burned CDs from my emo phase: Brand New's *Your Favorite Weapon*, Taking Back Sunday's *Tell All Your Friends*, and all the Dashboard Confessional I could bootleg from LimeWire.

Henry and I were having so much fun singing along to snippets of songs, I missed his exit three times. When we finally arrived back at his apartment complex, I waited expectantly for him to kiss me. When he didn't make his move, I thought maybe it was like the phone call, and

I leaned in to kiss him. He swerved his face away. "It takes more than one night to get a kiss from me, darling," he chided.

"But you've kissed me already!"

"You were crying."

"Not when you kissed me."

Henry just shrugged and stepped out of the car. Three days would pass before the scent of his cologne faded from the upholstery.

From the same places I'd learned that all men want is sex, I'd also been taught that a man who doesn't attempt to bed you immediately must want more than your body. I wasn't going to marry my high school sweetheart, but maybe I'd walk down the aisle with this gentle-man I'd met under the watchful gaze of a cartoon shark. This is what the romance plot had promised me. Henry was a sign from the universe that there was still hope, that I could still follow the formula for forever love and find my happily ever after, that I'd survived heartbreak because there was something more meant for me.

Henry would hold my hand. Pull out my chair. Help me into my coat after he paid for dinner. But never anything more than that. He contin-ued to send me "I hope you're smiling wherever you are" texts. Often, I would be. Many times, I'd be with another man.

Henry didn't seem to mind the other men or hearing about them. Because our relationship was platonic, I didn't instate my typical "Don't Ask, Don't Tell" policy that I exercised with the multiple men I was dat-ing (I didn't want to hear about other women any more than I imagined they wanted to hear about the rest of my rotation). Potentially, at first, I might have expected jealousy to spur Henry to make a move, but once it became clear he wasn't bothered, it was just another part of telling him about what I'd been doing since the last time he'd seen me. Unlike me struggling to come to terms with how I fit into Henry's life, he was secure about his place in mine. He simply wasn't possessive. Once, he asked me what I was doing, and I texted back that I was bowling. He'd correctly assumed I was at the bougie lanes by his place. His next text popped up: "I'm outside. Do you want to go for ice cream?"

I explained that I was on a triple date—but yes, I wanted to go get ice cream. My whack date had looked at me expectantly when the cashier rang us up for five-dollar-lane night and didn't buy me a drink even as his boys headed over to the bar to buy drinks for my girls. I had no problem leaving my date to be a fifth wheel with his friends and mine. And I didn't give him my number when he asked for it, walking alongside me for a few feet as I floated toward Henry. I was forever floating toward Henry.

Henry would party with my friends and me, and he'd buy the whole crew drinks, even though he didn't drink. Because Henry always dressed in designer labels, one of my friends liked to call him "Mr. GQ." When we went shopping, he'd insist I sit inside the dressing room with him, watching him remove one shirt, then put on another. When we went grocery shopping, he'd tell me to grab the items on the highest shelf. As I went up on my tippy-toes in a short skirt, he'd admire me and say, "I love to watch you reach." Eventually, Henry would find that he had enough room in his Sundays for the Lord and me. He was the only Catholic I knew who attended evening Mass. I'd pick him up after services to go to dinner, or sometimes I'd drop him off after gallivanting around Orange County all day together. He'd linger by the open car door, employing all of his suave to get me to attend with him. I never did.

I'm not a believer. As a kid, I peeked during grace and was disappointed not to see Jesus's bright white feet hovering above the dinner table, his hair rippling in a nonexistent breeze. I asked too many questions in Sunday school. One of the main benefits of getting my own car at sixteen was that I didn't have to "pray in the new year" with my aunt and cousins anymore. I'd just never gotten that tingle in my chest that told me God was real. He certainly hadn't saved my parents' marriage, although I remember my mother devotedly hauling us to Mass throughout the early years of my childhood, her hands cramping from hours of doing the hair of three curly-headed little girls and putting us in ruffle dresses with ruffle undies and matching ruffle socks.

By that point in our friendship, I would have followed Henry down any dark corridor, behind any locked door; I would have fallen into bed with him; but I couldn't follow him into faith. So, I added this as a reason why our relationship was missing a sexual element. When we went out in Hollywood and I found him outside, chatting up a Japanese girl who looked as bored as I had the first night we met and knowing he had an ex in Tokyo, I added my Blackness to that list, too. When he asked me late one night to drive him to Marina Del Rey to console a friend—and she expected us to relate to the struggles of sitting at a luxury car dealership while waiting for the money transfer from her parents to clear—I mentally jotted down my absence of familial wealth. I saw Henry's lack of sexual interest as rejection, and the cause of that rejection needed to be defined—so that I could correct it with Henry, or avoid it with the next man, or better understand whose love I was unworthy of. That time would have been better spent seeking self-acceptance. But the romance formula doesn't rely on self-acceptance; it seeks acceptance outwardly. Sex is an essential step, even when the camera (or the writer) glances away from the act. The rules dictate that sex without love is meaningless and love without sex is unrequited. A marriage without physical intimacy is called loveless, called a bed death, not far removed from a deathbed.

But it was also Henry's refusal of physical intimacy that'd allowed us to get so close. Allowed me to develop a relationship with him that didn't involve getting drunk to silence my fears of what could happen when alone with a man. I became comfortable in the absolute knowledge that, like I had experienced in gay bars, we could hold hands and flirt and be close, and I'd never be in danger of anything more happening, of anything unwanted happening.

Even so, I had a hard time understanding why Henry's love wasn't accompanied by physical attraction. My friends and I probably discussed the possibility he was gay, but it's not like that would have made our relationship make more sense. It wasn't like he was parading me around his friends and family as a beard. I'd met few people in his life. And asexuality wasn't really a conversation anyone was having at the time. Regardless of the reason, it felt like Henry and I were role-playing a relationship and not really living one. Like we were an old-timey sitcom couple regaling the world with our happy marriage every week and then retreating to our separate twin beds every night. Our sitcom marriage performed well for audience ratings, but when no one was there to watch, our relationship was an empty set.

I wasn't some horndog frat boy pressuring Henry to fuck me. It wasn't really about the lack of sex. The lack of sex was just the most visible element of the incompleteness between us. It was more tangible than the emotional depth that was also missing. I could only be happy in this house of love Henry and I had built until I tried to really live in it and discovered the cabinet doors didn't open and the appliances were props.

One night, on the way back to Henry's apartment, I wanted to know why he rarely talked about himself. I wanted to know why he went out with my friends, but I'd never been out with his. Why he'd become online friends with my sister after telling me he didn't have Facebook. Why. Why. Why.

In response, he teased me about falling in love with him.

"I'm not in love with you, Henry."

"Darling, a good thief can steal the key to your heart without you noticing it's gone missing."

We arrived at the gate to his apartment complex. Henry leaned over me to slide his key card into the reader. Whenever I came to pick him up, he'd come down to let me into the complex. Many months into the future, he'd finally tell me the reader was a fake. Any card slid into the slot would press the trigger that opened the gate. But this was not that night. I still had to wait on Henry to gain access.

When Henry put his hand on the car door to open it and leave, again without kissing me, I leaned across the space between us and kissed him. His body stiffened, then relaxed. Like the night we met, the kiss did not grow in intensity. I pulled away. Henry told me good night and left just like he always did. We never discussed the kiss. I'd gone from a girl who didn't text first to one who'd kiss a boy who had refused to kiss her.

As a woman, I assumed that men didn't fear me and my body the way I feared theirs. Most of them had power that I did not have. The almost certain power to physically protect their bodies from the sexual desires of women. I never thought about it consciously, but definitely, on some level, I must have believed that an uninterested man would stop me. I didn't consider that men can also freeze when uncomfortable. Or that the lie society tells us about men constantly wanting *"that thing, that thing"* is almost as flagrant as the one we're given about women asking for it when they clearly were not. I had put a friend in the position of choosing between accepting my actions or having to put his hands on a woman in a way that he might not be OK with in order to restrain me. I had allowed men to kiss me, and even more, because it'd been easier or felt safer than refusing. Yet, I couldn't recognize their entitlement in my own behavior. This is how rape culture uses us all. Men drowning in a pool of it, women choking on a sip of it.

I couldn't figure Henry out. He wanted to date me but not kiss me. He wanted me to desire him, and he praised my beauty, but he didn't want to do anything more than look—never touch. There was no Harlequin plot for this. I didn't have any friends who'd been through this. This was not a known variant of the happily-ever-after formula. But how many times had that formula failed to produce actual happiness? I could look at my parents and the parents of most of the people I knew. I could look at myself and most of my friends, freshly single post-college. Was Henry presenting me with something that existed outside of a traditional relationship dynamic? Was what we had even a relationship? We were like some contemporary spin on *When Harry Met Sally*. Can a man and a woman be more than friends without a lack of sex getting in the way?

Consent isn't just about physical acts. Henry and I needed to be clearer about the relationship we expected the other to partake in. We were each just performing a role and hoping the other person was willing to abandon their script for ours. My script resembled the one I'd believed everyone else was following about how a relationship should progress. And only Henry knew what his script read. He'd refused to break character, not even long enough to explain to me what role he had cast me in. If I still believed in tossing pennies into fountains, I'd have closed my eyes and wished for Henry's every thought.

Chapter 8

POTENTIAL

I met Chevy in a small bar in downtown Santa Ana right around the same time that I met Henry. He was wearing a thick, probably fake gold chain and lounging on a pleather couch. I was a few feet away on the dance floor. We were the only two Black people in the bar, and where I'm from, that meant you spoke, you nodded, you acknowledged each other. But I was learning that Orange County Black folk can act funny. I'd need a different in with him. When he got up to go to the restroom, I waited a few minutes, then followed.

I caught him in the hallway on his walk back and stepped in his way. He tried to step around me, thinking my move was unintentional. I stepped back into his path and looked up at him. He was a whole foot taller than me. I know it wasn't that original, but I asked him, "So, when you going to dance with me?"

On the dance floor, he asked for my number and told me he was a rapper. Later that night, I texted him a few bars, half joking, mostly flirting. My little freestyle wasn't memorable, but I was.

The next time I saw him, Chevy met up with me outside a bar near his place in Fullerton. "Wow. You're pretty," he said when he saw me. I was confused; he reminded me I wasn't dressed up the night we met. I'd been wearing a tank top with a strap held in place by a jumbo safety pin and shoes I'm almost ashamed to describe—Supra sneakers with gold glitter and a gold snake print. Gawd, he hated those shoes.

"If I was dressed so awful, why'd you get my number?" I asked him as we sat under a streetlight and watched groups of girls in colorful club attire flit past us like schools of fish. It was spring, but the air that night was already that perfect summer warm that reminds you of being young and directionless.

He shrugged. "You had potential."

In Chevy, I saw potential, too. Potential for my next great romance. Then, Chevy told me that I'd never be his girlfriend. "I always cheat on them," he explained. The bill on his fitted black Dodgers cap made it hard for me to look him in the eyes.

I didn't take Chevy at his word. The first time I went to his house, I came with a baking sheet and cookie dough because it was too hot to bake at mine and his place had AC. His roommates were smitten. Upstairs, in his room, there was cardboard on his wall that his friends had tagged with spray paint. His clothes were neatly hung, his shoes in an orderly row in his closet. Nothing on the floor. Bed made.

We didn't get any further than making out because I was on my period. Chevy immediately lost interest. He sat up and began putting on his shoes. "I'm going to the studio." I'm not sure if I said anything, probably a weak little "Oh."

I followed Chevy down the stairs and out onto the sidewalk. An elderly white couple were walking up the block toward us. We heard the *chuck-chuck* sound of the locks jamming down on their beat-up old Honda, which they were clearly walking toward. Chevy and I exchanged a look to confirm we'd just been the victims of a racist act. He pulled out his key fob and aimed it at a car just past the Honda as the couple approached. The headlights on his Audi blazed to life.

The next time I saw Chevy, I was not on my period. I'd texted and called him a gazillion times from my friend's house party. I was so drunk that I'd tried to slide across the edge of a Ping-Pong table some people were playing beer pong on, and it collapsed when I hit the middle. All the red Solo cups rushed downward, a waterfall of beer. I had to have one of my girls run me home so I could shower and change.

When Chevy arrived, I led him back to the hostess's bedroom. He didn't have a condom, but my friend had placed a plate of them in the bathroom. He returned with a Magnum. I liked to call them golden tickets.

Afterward, I curled up on the couch in the living room. He asked me if I was all right. "Yeah, just leave. I'm sleepy." I rolled over to face the back of the couch. He left. Back then, that was sufficient. Now, there's so much conversation—necessary conversation—around consent and whether or not you can give it after you've been drinking heavily, especially if your partner isn't as drunk as you are. It wouldn't be the same these days. All I know is that back then, I never felt weird the next morning after drunken, near-blackout sex with Chevy. Or anyone else.

In my twenties, every alcohol-doused dalliance that didn't violate my vague definition of consensual sex confirmed that what the boy from around the corner had done was not my fault. I smashed through all the rules. I was drunk. I was in a short skirt. I invited men I hardly knew into my bed. And those men didn't hold me down. Didn't ignore my tears. Didn't rape me. I took those risks, slammed my body against the wall of propriety over and over, expecting to shatter, but I never did.

Henry only wanted to date, and Chevy only wanted to fuck. And between them both, it was almost like I had a whole boyfriend. It became a routine with Chevy and me. I'd get drunk; I'd call him; he'd scoop me up from the bar and then drive me home to hook up. I saved so much money on taxis. My girls always grimaced when he arrived. He was standoffish, and when he did speak, it was often to say something jerky to one of us.

When a friend—who's older than me and a therapist—asked me about my attraction to Chevy, I told her, "He has this sadness. And I want to take some of it for him." She was too polite to tell me that what I'd said was, um, unhealthy, but her eyes didn't lie.

Still, Chevy was reliable for a ride and good in bed. When I asked him how he got so good, he said, "I watched a lot of that *Real Sex* doc on HBO when I was a kid."

Chevy had rules. He never stayed after sex. He never went down on me. And he never wanted to hear about anything happening in my life. If he couldn't come to get me when the bars closed, he'd listen to my tipsy chatter on the phone at 2:00 a.m. He rarely sent me to voice mail. Like he'd promised, I never became his girlfriend, but the girls who *did* didn't like my calls. And those girlfriends probably liked our drunk sex even less. After a while, I stopped caring about them. I'd been there first, and I'd be there after they were gone, too.

I'd probably known Chevy for three years before I learned even basic things about him, like his last name and that he had a brother. One night he was being lenient. I no longer lived with the three boys. I'd recently moved into a two-bedroom apartment with a friend of a friend. I'd invited him over to my new place with a pic of an AriZona Iced Tea, a Black & Mild, and a Magnum—a few of his favorite things. I captioned the pic "Rapper trap." As I strutted around my bedroom in some stilettos he'd wanted to see me in, I mentioned the promotion I'd gotten at my new job and a grad school admittance I'd received but ultimately decided not to take. "I didn't know you cared about that kind of thing," he said.

I stopped strutting. My ambition had always been a defining characteristic. No one who knew me would be surprised by these things. But Chevy didn't know me, not really. He only knew me as the drunk chick he picked up after last call. Even when we hung out at my place, we mostly just talked about mixtapes or watched *The Boondocks*. Your twenties are probably the only time that you can be as into someone as I was into Chevy without actually having any deep conversations about anything.

That night, Chevy went down on me for the first time and was still beside me in bed when morning came. Our first time together in broad daylight. He looked me in the eyes, touched my cheek, and said, "Good. You still look pretty without makeup on." How romantic.

Periodically, feelings for Chevy would swell up inside me. If I ever tried to talk to him about us being more than what we were, he wasn't having it. I treated his affection like a Rubik's Cube. If I did this or said that, twisted this way or that way, maybe I'd unlock his feelings for me. I found the more distant I became, the closer to me he wanted to be. So, I strategically kept my distance and continued to date other men.

Chapter 9

CAMP PENDLETON IS THE SIZE OF RHODE ISLAND

A year and a summer after I met Henry, my roommate and I drove down to the Del Mar racetrack for its annual beer and reggae festival. The August 2010 headliner was Matisyahu. The track is just north of San Diego. For a Louisville girl who'd grown up with the twin spires of Churchill Downs pricking the sky above her and its lawns of the finest bluegrass cushioning the ground beneath her, Del Mar's patchy turf and synthetic track were less than impressive. But I wasn't there for horse racing.

Carrie and I walked around the grounds with frothy gold brew in our Solo cups. It was that gilded hour before the sun takes one last long, hot look over the horizon, then slowly sinks into the ocean, and the day cools to night. Matisyahu was about to take the stage. I dislike standing at the front of a concert, pressed up against strangers, so we stayed back where the crowd had feathered out a bit.

A group of guys stood not too far from us, and one of them looked like someone I'd actually want to be pressed up against. I nudged Carrie. She nodded her approval. I could tell by the stiff way they held their bodies they were military men, and Carrie, Carrie had a thing for military men. She liked the clean-cutness of a man in uniform and the security that government benefits provided. Both of us short and curvy, we focused our energy on the men, and she ran a hand through her chin-length black hair and threw the guys a classic come-hither look. They responded immediately.

The white boys crowded around Carrie, and her pale cheeks flushed from the attention. The only Black boy in the crew—the one I'd noticed—chose to speak to me. He told me his name was Flash. Flash like lightning. Like that feeling that zips up the spine when eyes meet for the first time, followed by that quick snap of the future, of what could be. He said he was from Brooklyn by way of Jamaica.

He was 5'9" with a body chiseled by Uncle Sam and skin so brown, it made the surrounding adobe buildings look washed out. "Where you fro—" he'd begun to ask me. But just then, there was a commotion in the crowd, and he and his friends dashed off into the fray as a single unit. Their knees rising and landing in time together, I could picture them in their combat boots. They reemerged, hauling a man who was having an asthma attack—possibly triggered by the weed smoke that coiled upward into the night air. He didn't have his inhaler. The guys got him seated on the ground and guided him through deep-breathing exercises until the attack passed. He thanked them repeatedly, grabbing each of their hands in turn and shaking vigorously. And when the men began walking back toward Carrie and me, they had the strut of heroes in their step.

Flash led me away from our friends and through the crowd. He used an arm to guide people out of his path and, when necessary, used his bulk to move them over. This made me feel cared for, protected, *delicate*. So, I readily gave Flash my hand and let him pull me closer to the stage. He stopped a third of the way from the front of the crowd, then asked me, "Can you see OK?" I'm 5'3"; I can never "see OK" in a crowd, but I nodded yes anyway.

The sky completely dark, Matisyahu walked onto the stage with a full beard and wearing a yarmulke. The curls dangling at his temples bounced with his every step. He flicked his right arm at his band, a signal to begin. He wrapped his fingers around the mic, and Flash wrapped his arms around my waist. He held me so tightly that again I felt delicate, but this time, fragile, stifled. I blamed the beer for his forwardness and for why I allowed it.

Single for over a year, I'd grown jealous watching couples hugged up at concerts. I missed that feeling of closeness. So, I decided to pretend I shared that feeling with Flash, a guy I'd known for less than an hour. To pretend just for the night that I had that thing back, that thing my ex and I had once shared. And when Flash turned me around to kiss me, full on mashing his face into mine, lapping at the inside of my mouth with his beer-sodden tongue, I pretended that too was a thing I was ready to share with him.

I sat on the floor, the carpet itching against my thighs, with my back against my bed and my phone on speaker. Flash repeated his request: "Promise me you won't forget about me. Promise." His unit was going to run some drills in the wilds of San Diego for a week. He'd wanted to see me again right away, have a proper date, but this had come up unexpectedly.

"A week isn't nearly long enough to forget someone, Flash." Nor was knowing someone a week nearly long enough for making such desperate pleas, but there Flash was on the other end of my phone, pleading with me to remember him.

"Well, then promise me you won't run off with some other man while I'm gone. I'll be thinking about you." It was nice to hear someone say they'd be thinking about me when I wasn't around. Chevy only thought about me in the few hours of friendship we offered each other late at night. I was free of the emotional burden of worrying about Chevy's life choices, but that also meant he wasn't there to support mine or lift me up when I needed it. Maybe that's what Flash was offering.

I promised I wouldn't forget him. We made plans to spend the following Saturday at the beach on base.

I'd been waiting at the Camp Pendleton gate for close to an hour when I saw a soldier in my rearview mirror taking strong, solid steps toward my car; his hands clutched the assault rifle he wore slung across his body. The flat black weapon cut a clean outline against his sand-and-dust-colored fatigues. It was the guard's third trip over to check on me. "Ma'am, how's it going? He still coming for you?"

The guard wore an easy smile, but I was eye level with his firearm.

"Yes, sir, he just called and said he went to the wrong gate." The guard flexed a larger smile, then headed back to his station.

Flash had asked me to arrive at 11:00 a.m.; because he was in the military, I assumed that 11:00 a.m. meant 11:00 a.m. But when I called him to say I'd arrived at the gate, he wasn't ready. "Already? Sorry! Fifteen minutes—just got to shower."

Thirty minutes went by, and then he called to tell me he had to find a ride. Then he realized I wasn't at the main gate. I was annoyed. "I asked you for directions! You said just use my GPS. This is where my GPS led me."

"You've just got to drive around to the main gate," he said.

I decided I'd rather drive home. I pulled a U-turn and gave the guard a wave goodbye. All that anger in me needed a release. I imagined myself ripping up the 5 freeway back to Orange County, but there was so much traffic, my car hardly moved. Every few minutes, my phone lit up with a call or a text from Flash. After fifteen minutes in the same spot, I gave in and answered.

He was pleading with me again. "I'll make it up to you. Just come back. We'll do lunch."

At the main gate of Camp Pendleton, Flash ran over to my car. He had on shiny purple Nikes, a purple T-shirt, black jeans, and a lightweight black jacket. At least he looked good. He opened my car door and mashed his face into mine, again. When I pushed him off me, I could smell him on my lips. Flash had arrived at my car fully clothed for our first date, but he'd rushed past all my boundaries in a way halfclothed Henry would never.

"Hey, I'm mad at you," I said.

"I'm sorry," he said, but he was grinning.

He showed his badge to the guard, and I was allowed to drive through the gate.

"What's for lunch?" I asked.

"Oh, we'll just hit up the food court on base."

I pushed lo mein around on my plate until it was time for the beach. The meal had been far from "making it up" to me.

The beach was clean, free of litter and ocean debris—no knots of kelp or pieces of driftwood. In the distance, a line of marines jogged across the sand, their sweat-slicked abs glinting in the sunlight.

I asked Flash where I could change into my suit. "In the car," he said.

I wished I had worn my suit so I wouldn't have to change in front of him. I hitched up my maxi-dress, inched down my panties, and wriggled on my bikini bottom the best I could without exposing myself. When I looked over, he was watching me. "Stoooooop!"

"Why?" he asked.

"Because it's rude."

When Henry invited me into dressing rooms with him, it was as if he'd wanted me to watch. To see my face in the reflection of the mirror as he admired his own body. Double adulation. But I had not invited Flash to brazenly admire my body.

Flash turned his head. I could see his eyes straining to watch me. When we got out of the car, it only took him a few minutes to undress down to his swim trunks.

There were other couples and families around, but the beach was mostly empty. We laid out on my towel.

Flash threw an arm over me and said, "I'm glad you came back; it's nice being here with you."

Lulled by the warmth of the sun and the salty breeze, my frustration dissipated.

Flash told me about joining the marines, growing up in New York, and how he was off to Okinawa next. "Yeah, all the white boys teased me because I kept failing the swim test in basic and almost didn't make it. They asked me how I grew up with all that water but didn't know how to swim, so I asked them how they grew up with all this land but didn't know how to run."

As he talked, he sprinkled sand along my legs. "You have amazing thighs," he said.

"Thanks, I eat a lot of ice cream."

"I wish ice cream did that to my body." How he looked at me as his hand crept up my thigh made me uneasy. I shifted on the towel so his hand would topple off my leg. Minutes later, his hand found its way back. I made my intentions clearer: "Stop being so touchy-feely."

I was playful in my approach, careful not to offend him. Careful not to stoke his fury or his desire.

He moved his hand to my face. "You're beautiful. I like being here with you, and I know I'll miss you when I leave for Japan, but I want to get to know you anyway. OK?" He nodded at me, and I found myself reflexively nodding back. "After this, we'll go see a movie, then grab a bottle and have some alone time."

"I don't know." I placed my hand over his hand.

"What? You don't drink?"

"We met at a beer festival. It's the 'alone time' I don't know about." He smiled at me and mussed my hair.

"Hey!" I shouted and immediately went to work fixing it. When he spoke again, he was asking me about living in Orange County and how I came to be there.

After an hour or so, he told me it was time to go. He gave me directions back to the main gate. On the way, he pointed out his barracks. Off base, he let the GPS on his phone handle the directions, and I followed the turns called out by a snobby English voice. "You have arrived at your destination."

"Where's the theater?" I asked.

"Just turn here," he said.

"Turn where?" I craned my neck around and didn't see a theater anywhere. I didn't see a movie marquee. I didn't see a massive parking lot filled with cars. I didn't see families leaving, holding hands, munching on popcorn. All I saw was a strip of sleazy motels. It was 3:00 p.m., their neon vacancy signs Easter-egg pastel in the sunlight.

"Just choose any of these," he said with a wave of his hand.

My mouth went dry, and my palms went wet against the steering wheel. My eyes met with Flash's eyes; this time, a different feeling zipped up my spine, a different snap of the future, of what he could be.

"I don't want to hang out in a motel room with you."

"Why not?" He asked like he had a right to, like my body language hadn't given him all the answers he needed, like I hadn't already spoken out against "alone time."

"Because I don't," I said out loud, but in my head, I completed the sentence: *want to be raped by you.*

It'd been nearly a decade since the boy from around the corner and the empty apartment he had after he graduated high school. Since the door shutting and locking behind me. Click.

When I'd first met Henry, I was nervous to let him in my car. Worried about how he might harm me. A year later, I hadn't hesitated to let Flash hop into the passenger seat. I'd worked my way from the linoleum at Henry's front door deeper into his apartment, snuggled up on his couch, flopped on his bed, and had even heckled him about the unusual amount of canned beans in his cupboard. Total comfort. Henry had never once transgressed my body. And other men benefited from how Henry's trustworthiness had dismantled my justified defenses. How many other men had been in my car? How many cars had I ridden in? How many beds had I fallen into? How many times had I shown up to meet a man at his home, no longer waiting for the sound of a click?

"Just park. Then get out of the car. Stop being so difficult." Flash rubbed my knee like I was a cat he could stroke into submission. I was still stopped in the middle of the road.

"It's too early to go to the movies. We'll just go in and wash the sand off," he continued. I lifted his hand from my knee and flung it back at him. I swung my car into the parking lot, pulled into a space, and kicked it into reverse, then shifted into drive again and sped back onto the road. My mind began listing how I was to blame for this: *I was drunk when I met him. I let him kiss me. I came back. I wore this dress with the cleavage. I-I-I-I.*

"Where are you driving?" Flash asked, laughing at me with all his teeth showing. The town next to the base, Oceanside, was like one big loop, and I didn't know how to get off the main road and back to Camp Pendleton.

"I'm going home."

He stopped laughing. "No, no, no. We can still go to the movies. Or just walk around Oceanside. It's too early to end our day."

"I'm going home."

"Then take me with you."

"That's too much driving," I said, wondering why I was still providing explanations.

I parked in the small visitor's lot off to the side of the main gate. I tried to be polite, not let my rage put me in even greater danger. I didn't know what else he was capable of. "I had a nice day at the beach. But now I'm ready to go home." I waited for him to get out of my car.

He reached over and removed my sunglasses. "The motel was a bad idea. I'm sorry. Let's not ruin things." I got the distinct feeling that he'd done this and worse to other girls. I was worried for the women of Okinawa.

I turned and stared straight ahead, my hands still wrapped around the steering wheel. "Get out of my car. Please."

Still facing me, he said, "No."

No, this was not my fault. This was all him. I began shoving at his legs and his chest while I screamed, "GETOUTOFMYCARGETOUTOFMYCARGETOUTOFMYCAR."

He was solid. Body chiseled by Uncle Sam. He didn't budge a bit. Calmly, he said, "No, I'm not leaving." Like many men, he saw *no* as his alone, refusing to accept mine no matter how strongly I insisted. "At least drive me back to my barracks."

Fun fact: Camp Pendleton is the size of Rhode Island.

I didn't remember the way to his barracks, and he'd already shown he couldn't be relied on for directions.

"No."

"But it's a five-mile walk back."

"That's not my problem."

My car felt smaller and smaller and smaller. Other cars were passing us as they entered and exited the base through the main gate. I saw a patrol car pull into the visitor's lot. A sailor in a green beret and desert fatigues emerged from the vehicle. Another sailor in a red beret walking across the parking lot stopped to chat with him.

I snatched Flash's phone from the center console, scrambled out of the car, ran around to his side, and swung his door open with full force. "Get the fuck out of my car before I scream." I figured if I screamed, the sailors in the berets would come over, and it would be a scene. He got out of the car and snatched his phone from me. I ran back around to the other side. He chased me, saying, "I need my jacket!"

I got into my car and reached over to pull the door closed, but he had wedged his thigh in between the car and the door. "I need my jacket!" he repeated.

I grabbed his jacket from the back seat and pushed it through the gap at him. He kept saying, "You don't have to do this. You don't have to do this."

When he bent over to pick up his jacket from the ground, I shouted at him, "I know. I want to," followed by an excellently timed door slam. When I hit the gas, he stumbled backward from the car to keep my tires from scuffing his shiny Nikes.

I could only make a right out of the parking lot, so I had to go through the main gate to turn around and get back onto the freeway. I explained this to the guard at the post. His eyes traveled down to the cleavage exposed by my sundress. The strap of the seat belt felt cool against my breastbone. "Really, you don't want to stay awhile?" he joked.

"No, I'll just be on my way," I said and did my best to cobble together a little smile. Still, after everything that had happened that afternoon, remaining polite was my most immediate instinct.

Flash called me over and over again for the entire two hours in traffic it took to get back to Orange County. I was so rattled I hadn't thought to turn my phone off. There were text messages about seeing me again, about how he was sorry, about how he would make it up next time.

When I pulled into my apartment complex, I reached down for my gate key; it wasn't there. I sat very still in my car and thought. Had Flash stolen my gate key? Had he seen the apartment complex parking permit sticker on my back windshield? Did he know where I lived? Was he coming for me? He was a marine, trained in skills I couldn't even imagine, and what I'd seen today was probably only the beginning. Was he calling to tell me he was en route to my place? I reached down again and squirmed my hand under my seat. My fingers flitted across something smooth and plastic. I inched the gate key out of the gap. It had probably been flung out of its place when I grabbed Flash's phone. He wasn't coming for me. But my mind had gone there. I was far, far away from him but scared enough that he was still in my system, warping my every thought for the worse.

HONK!

I jumped in my seat. A car had pulled up behind me and was waiting for me to pass through the gate.

I locked the front door and then my bedroom door, and I cocooned myself in blankets and sheets and pillows, finally feeling safe enough to relax. There was no part of me that wanted this to resolve like a fairy-tale romance, with Flash traversing every moat, castle wall, and barrier I'd put in place to dodge his dangerous affection. I sent off one tweet before shutting my eyes: "Wow. That was the worst afternoon of the summer."

Hours later, I shoved my pillows off me and pushed back my covers. I had a text from Henry. I hadn't heard from him in a few weeks. The last time he'd invited me to come to church with him, I grew so flustered by his invite that I got lost on my way home, a drive I'd done many times before. Usually, his invitation and my declining of his invitation felt routine, but one time, while he'd hovered with his arm slung over the open door and his head ducked into the car, he'd held direct eye contact with me for longer than usual. "C'mon, M," he'd said. I couldn't. We hadn't spoken since.

Henry's text read, "Honey, it can't be that bad! Won't you smile?" He'd seen my tweet.

I called him and told him the whole story. He agreed that it was that bad. "Sounds straight out of a movie. I can't believe that happened to you. Did you say you were wearing your bikini? The 'sex-inducing' one?" I had thought that joke was funny earlier in the summer when Henry and I had made plans to go to a pool party, but not anymore.

"Henry."

"Honey, I'm only joking! When things are this awful, all we can do is laugh. Come get me. I'll take you for a makeup date." I told him I wasn't up for it, and he said, "Well, at least ice cream, then."

Hours earlier, I had been trapped in my car with a potential date rapist, and now I was seated next to a man who'd refused to kiss me on our first date. "M, do you remember when we used to just drive around in your car?"

I pointed out that drifting around town and unintentionally passing his exit were not the same thing.

"Well, keep driving, anyway," he said. Henry gently patted my leg, and when we reached his exit, I missed the off-ramp on purpose. Henry periodically gave me directions, then told me to pull into what, to my relief, was not a motel but the parking lot of a closed restaurant. "We're going to Disney!"

We got out of the car. Henry placed his arm around my waist, and my head found its home against his heart. "That's too much money to spend when the park's closing so soon." Not to mention I hadn't been to Disneyland since Tyler and I had broken up.

"Oh, M, please? I've never been!" His arm moved from my waist to my shoulder, and he twirled a lock of my hair around his finger. Family after family passed us, exiting the park with children sleeping in their arms or snoozing in strollers. I knew Henry was lying about having never been. He was always inviting me to play in a fantasy more magical than my day-to-day.

I'd railed against myself earlier for not seeing the red flags with Flash, for trusting someone I should have known had bad intentions, but I'd once extended Henry the same kind of trust. If I hadn't overridden those early fear cues, there'd be no Henry and me. There'd be no nights like this.

"Henry, we'll go another time," I said, but we kept walking toward the park entrance.

Once we passed the checkpoint but before the ticketed entry to the actual park, there was a huge area between Disneyland and California Adventure. There were about fifty people seated on the ground, looking up at the sky expectantly.

"What are all these people here for?" I asked Henry as he guided me over to an empty space and coaxed me down to the ground with him. I sat in front of him, with his arms wrapped around me like a favorite sweater. A barrier between me and the night chill.

"They're here for the fireworks," he said. On cue, like magic, shooting stars made of fire zipped across the sky in streaks of spectacular white light. The fireworks burst onto the canvas of the night. This had been his plan all along. Henry held me close, occasionally kissing the side of my face and squeezing me tightly. There was a tingle in my chest. Henry and I weren't in Mass, and I still could not call myself a believer, but he had restored my faith.

Chapter 10

Knowing My Status

I prefer to see a woman gynecologist, but Dr. L's was the only practice in Laguna Beach. His proximity made it possible for me to squeeze an appointment in over a lunch break.

In college, I saw the same gyno as my mother. Once during an exam, he voiced his appreciation for my belly button ring, the blingy, dangly jewelry resting cold and cheap on my bare stomach. He never had a nurse in the room during my visits. And I was too young to know I could ask for one. At another appointment, I reminded him to do my breast exam—he'd skipped it last visit. He wondered aloud how he could forget my breasts, his tone warm and goopy, as if my tits were somehow precious to him. From the hallway, I could hear the clicking of nails, his wife's dog pawing at the shut exam room door. His wife kept an office at his practice and was in the next room at her desk. On my way out, unprompted, he began massaging my shoulders. I never went back. Neither did my mother.

I didn't report him because I didn't know how, but also, I worried that I'd invited his behavior. He'd once complained that earlier in his career, patients would send him thank-you notes, but not anymore—delivering babies had become a thankless task. As a kind gesture, I'd dropped a Christmas card in the mail, thanking him for being a good doctor. But evidently, he was not a good doctor or a good man.

The next gyno I chose to see when I was a college student was a woman. I informed her that per my previous doctor, I needed an exam every six months. Something about my family medical history. No, she told me, that wasn't true.

I began seeing Dr. L when I moved to Orange County. His office had a fish tank in the waiting room. Current magazines filled with the freshest celeb gossip. Exam tables with velour booties over the metal stirrups—no cold feet. But what I appreciated most were the cotton gowns. Many gynecologists' offices expect their patients to change into an open-front paper sheath dress. To replicate this experience, rub a crumpled sheet of printer paper across your nipples and see if it puts you in the mood for medical care. Sometimes, it's just a boxy, open-front vest made out of the same waxy-plasticky material as the bib they clip around you at the dentist's office.

Once you're in your paper gown, they tell you to hop up on the exam table, where they've unrolled more paper, like it's a butcher block and you're a choice cut ready to be wrapped up. Your paper-covered ass and the paper-covered table exchange crinkles. You sound like something someone has crushed up and discarded. Cotton gowns and white sheets are more humane. The cotton gowns, the velour booties, the fresh magazines are why I continued to see Dr. L, even after I didn't work in Laguna Beach any longer.

I undress at the gyno's like I'm a guest in someone's home. I slide my shoes under the chair in the exam room so no one trips over them. I neatly fold my clothes, careful to stack my garments in a way that conceals my bra and panties. As if modesty matters there.

Dr. L is what I imagine a Ken doll would look like if dolls aged. Forties. Friendly. He could've just as easily been my cashier at Target. He had the same level of checkout professionalism. Speedy without rushing. He scanned my items without comment.

We made our once-a-year small talk while he spelunked around in my vagina. His eye contact was with my nether regions, mine with the ceiling. Our conversation, somehow, led us to the topic of fame. "I couldn't be a celebrity," he said. "No privacy."

"I know what you mean," I said, throwing my voice forward in the direction of the white sheet spread across my knees, shielding his face from view. His comment reminded me of my first gyno visit. When my period began at fourteen, my cramps were so painful, I'd faint. My mother insisted I needed to go to the doctor. My father decided that he had to escort me to my appointment in a show of support. That the entire family had to go with me. Including my two younger sisters. We all had breakfast at a restaurant beforehand. When the nurse called my name, my mother and I both stood. I told her I wanted to do the exam alone. I'd had enough family time. As the nurse led me back, my father called after us, "Don't be too invasive!"

The doctor was a small elderly man who advised that I should be put on birth control to manage my period. My father didn't like that idea. Instead, most months, I missed a day or two of school, in bed with cramps. And kept a spare pair of pants in my locker for accidents, like a not-fully-potty-trained kindergartner. My period regularly flooded tampons and gushed through pads.

As an eighteen-year-old freshman in college, I was old enough to put myself on birth control. When I returned to the gyno office, the small elderly man had retired, his practice passed to the belly-button-ring admirer. Initially, I chose a vaginal ring, thinking it'd be easier to keep up with than remembering to take a daily pill. After a few months, my vagina closed up around the ring like a tight, dry fist. I switched to the pill. Birth control cost me fifty dollars per month. For the pleasure of not getting me pregnant, I asked Tyler to split the expense with me. He did so without complaint.

With Tyler no longer around to subsidize my sex life, I was fortunate that Dr. L was generous with the birth control sample packs left behind by pharmaceutical reps. He'd give me months' worth for free every year.

"All done." The casters on Dr. L's short stool rattled as he rolled back from the exam table. I exhaled in relief. The Pap smear is the longest two minutes in reproductive health.

I lifted my heels out of the stirrups and sat up with the white sheet scrunched around my waist. Dr. L tapped the foot pedal on the trash can and dropped his soiled gloves in. He started to leave, saying, "Meet me in my office. I'll get your birth control prescription ready."

I almost didn't ask. I'd never asked a gynecologist before.

"Wait, um, can I get an STI screen?"

I'd also never been asked by a doctor if I wanted one. Maybe because Tyler and I had been together for years, gynos didn't think it was necessary. Or maybe it was because Kentucky is in the Bible Belt. Yes, I'd asked for birth control—and I'd had a fair bit of trepidation when making that request the first time, too—but it wasn't the same. I'd been within the confines of a long-term, committed relationship. And it was easy to tell myself, and the doctor, that it was more about my cramps than all the teenage sex I was having. In the back seat of cars. In parking garages. In my dorm room (of course, all with my boyfriend, who I planned on being with forever).

Asking Dr. L to renew a prescription I already had for birth control was easy. But asking him for an STI screen was hard for me. Because it was also a proclamation that I *needed* an STI screen. In the year since I'd last seen Dr. L, I'd probably slept with six or eight men. I was a kid who came up in the girl-power era, but watching the Spice Girls stomp around in platforms and spangled bras hadn't taught me true sexual empowerment, just how to perform it. I wasn't alone. A lot of young women I knew were sexually liberated but often ashamed to talk about that liberation outside the comfort of their friends. We kept our sex lives secret from our families. Our partners. Even our doctors. We let them all assume our numbers were low. If you were going to be a slut, the least you could do was be polite about it. Was politeness always doing the bidding of shame?

The STI screening conundrum: getting tested is a sexually responsible act viewed as evidence of sexual recklessness. *What have you been doing to make one necessary?*

I fretted: *No one wants to think about their little girl all used up. Men don't want to know your number. Your doctor will treat you like a slut if they know you're a slut.*

The negative messaging that rang inside my head almost didn't allow me to ask. I mean, in my defense, I did have a history with a gynecologist who saw a Christmas card from a woman young enough to be his daughter as an invitation to be a perv—fuck the Hippocratic oath, right?

"Sure," Dr. L said, "we can use this same sample." If Dr. L was judging me, it didn't show.

"For everything?"

"Everything except HIV. We'd need to draw blood for that."

"I have a thing about needles," I said.

By *thing*, I meant severe phobia. When I had to finish up a series of vaccines my senior year of high school, it took my mother and three nurses to hold me down while the doctor jammed the shot in my arm. I avoided having anything else drawn or injected for a straight decade.

"You don't need one anyway," Dr. L said. "Are you sleeping with someone who goes to Vegas every weekend to have unprotected sex with tons of people?" This seemed extreme, but maybe because his practice was in Laguna Beach, some of his patients could afford to indulge in weekly sex-based travel. Surely there were scenarios I could get into within county lines that would make an HIV test the responsible choice.

I wondered if this was the same advice given out at the Planned Parenthood minutes from where I lived in Costa Mesa. I'd gone there once, thinking it'd be less pressure to ask strangers than my usual doctor to test me. There was no fish tank in the lobby. It was crowded. Someone was crying. The underfunded clinic was so overbooked, the receptionist told me you just had to show up and wait to be seen. I looked at a young couple gripping each other's hands who looked like they'd cut class to be there. The girl, pregnant, was clearly in pain. I didn't stay.

Dr. L answered on my behalf by shaking his head no. Then, he left me alone in the exam room to get dressed. But the truth was, I didn't know what any of the people I'd slept with were doing when they weren't sleeping with me.

The last person I'd slept with was Chevy. I had no idea what his life was like outside of the occasional time block from 2:00 a.m. to 3:00 a.m. he spent in my bed. I knew more about his thoughts on the latest Drake album than I did about his day-to-day.

The last time we'd fucked, he'd been different. Tender, even. He wasn't behind me, roping the long locks of my hair around his fist or slamming his palm against the side of my ass. We were in missionary. He moved slow. When it was over, he laid a bridge of kisses across my collarbone.

I watched him pull his clothes back on. In my own haste to undress, I never saw him folding his clothes, but he always did—his T-shirt and jeans in neat little squares on my floor, as if he'd packed an invisible suitcase. He sat on the edge of my bed and slipped on his shoes. The quiet felt thick, meaningful. This felt like a goodbye, and I didn't know why.

So, the next day, I creeped him online.

I started with his Myspace page—even in 2010, the site was still popular for sharing music—and played his newest track. He was rapping about a girlfriend. It could have been old material, but his Twitter confirmed it: he'd sent out a tweet about a birthday gift he'd just bought her. I had no claim over Chevy, but I felt like I deserved to be informed he was seeing someone seriously. I wanted it to be my choice whether I participated in his cheating or not. But mostly, my feelings were hurt that there was a girl he wanted to be with, and that girl wasn't me.

I closed my laptop. His song, still playing in one of my open tabs, ended abruptly.

About a month after my annual exam, I was in bed, messing around online. My Twitter feed was saturated with HIV stats for March's Women and Girls HIV/AIDS Awareness Day. My virtual acquaintances tweeted out their statuses—noticeably, only those who'd tested negative. Meanwhile, I continued to tweet about rappers. The HIV stats were mostly information I knew, but there was one tweet that was news to me: "African American women are the fastest growing demographic for new HIV cases. They represent 67% of all new cases among women."

As it turned out, despite what Dr. L thought, I was exactly who needed to be tested. Unwilling to pay another co-pay for a do-over visit to the gyno, I told myself I'd tack an HIV test onto next year's annual exam. That gave me twelve months to overcome my fear of needles.

❤

My inability to say no to a free drink was how I found myself at a bar in downtown Fullerton, thirty minutes from home, drunk in the presence of people I hardly knew, on a work night. North of Anaheim, downtown Fullerton is a cluster of bars within walking distance of Fullerton College and a short drive from Cal State Fullerton. Thursday is a popular night to party for college kids who don't have classes on Fridays and, I guess, twentysomethings like me who were more concerned about having a good night than a good morning.

It was my first time out with one of my coworkers from the job I'd landed a year earlier as a smartphone rep. He and his friends chose the bar. I arrived later than they did, but it was still too early in the night to tell what the crowd was going to be like. The DJ was warming up by playing B sides and songs that were past their prime. The playlist might as well have been titled "Ludacris Revisited." We huddled in the crook of the L-shaped bar, calling out drinks to the bartender. This dude in the crew told her to put all the drinks on his tab. My coworker whispered to me, "He lives at home, so he always burns money at the bar."

There was champagne. There were shots of Henny. There were more shots. There was a Stella. There was a Corona. There was me too drunk to drive. It'd gotten too late to call someone. My friends were probably at home in bed, where I should've been, because they had work in the morning, just like I did.

My coworker got me a glass of water, and I glumly stood in the middle of the bar, sipping it. My phone vibrated in my hand—a text from a guy I'd been flirting with for weeks, "wyd 2nite, beautiful? Want to go out?" I texted back I was out already and "henny + beer = drrrizunk." He responded that he would hit me up over the weekend.

Phone already out, I shot Chevy the first text I'd sent him in months, "Drunk in Fullerton. Wish you still lived here." I hadn't hit him up since discovering his girlfriend, but I couldn't afford the long cab ride home. Contacting him was the most responsible idea out of a long list of irresponsible things I'd considered doing.

Right away he texted back, "Where at? We're in Fullerton, too."

Surprised, I responded, "Commonwealth. You and your girl?"

"Nah, my friend Chris. We're headed to you."

The dude running up a tab swung by with another flute of champagne and tried to press it into my hand; I waved him off and texted back, "Hurry!! Dude is trying to get me smashed."

The way a little kid gets during a Mickey Mouse sighting at Disney, that was me whenever I'd see Chevy. Exuberant joy. I rushed over to fling my arms around his waist and press my face into his plaid shirt. Predictably, he didn't return my affection. He hated any amount of PDA, any lack of restraint.

I greeted his friend Chris, and then Chris wandered off. Chevy leaned over me. "What you wearing? You can do better. I told Chris you were cute. I was hyping you up." It was a Thursday. I wasn't wearing anything special, but I definitely still looked cute in my striped miniskirt and baby tee. I certainly looked better than the night I'd picked Chevy up. I wanted to go off—he was being an asshole—but I needed something from him. I shrugged off his comment and pointed out I was dressed cute enough for some dude to have already bought me a hundred dollars' worth of drinks. I offered to buy Chevy and Chris a round.

"How you getting home?" Chevy asked.

"I dunno. I drove."

"Damn, Minda, you can't drive. You can come crash out at my place." He looked at me sternly. "And *just* crash out. I'm bound and determined to be just your friend."

I smirked. "But we are *just* friends."

He shook his head at me. Chris would drive himself home in Chevy's car so Chevy could drive us back to his place in my car. They'd meet back up the next day to get Chevy's car back to him. I was really impressed he was doing all that just so I didn't have to leave my car in downtown Fullerton, where they ticket you after a certain hour.

On the drive to his place, he stopped at a quickie mart to get water. From the car, I texted him, "GRAB SOME CONDOMS!" Because we both knew I wasn't just going to crash out at his place, and I was adamant about safe sex, even when drunk.

I closed my eyes for the rest of the ride to keep my nausea under control. When I got out of the car, I stared at my feet to block out the spinning world. I didn't raise my eyes until I was curled up on Chevy's bed. He'd moved since the last time I'd been to his place. His room was small but tidy. Beneath his shirts hanging in the closet, his shoes were still lined up two by two, like schoolchildren on a field trip.

Soon he was over me on the bed, and in mere seconds, I was down to my bra and panties. Black lace. It'd been a while since we'd been in this situation. Chevy paused to look at my body. He grazed my shoulder with his lips. "You have the softest skin I've ever felt."

"Guys tell me that a lot."

His eyes went from relaxed and dreamy to intense and direct. He probably didn't want to think about me with other guys. But if I had to wonder if I was sleeping on his girlfriend's side of the bed, I wanted him to know he wasn't the only one who had others.

I hitched my thighs high up on his hips, and he leaned into me. "How's your girlfriend feel about my soft skin?" I asked.

"She does her dirt, too," he murmured before kissing me.

The next morning, I opened my eyes. I was face to face with a burn hole in a naked mattress. The fitted sheet was rumpled up beneath my body and tangled around one of my arms. Tissue-thin curtains did nothing to tone down the sun. I closed my eyes for reprieve. When I opened them again, I was looking at wood paneling on the ceiling that'd been painted white. There was also brown wood paneling on the walls.

I told Chevy, who was beside me in bed, that I needed to leave. I was late for work.

He opened a door that led outside, and I stepped down three short steps. My car was parked under a carport attached to a mobile home. We were surrounded by mobile homes. "You moved to a trailer park?"

"It's this quiet all the time. Nothing but old people live here. I love it," he said. I looked around again; the homes were laid out like orderly rows of Lego. It did seem more peaceful than the place in Huntington Beach I'd inadvertently found myself at after answering that Craigslist ad with no photos.

I didn't ask Chevy why he moved. Just like the night before, I hadn't asked about his Audi when I saw him hand Chris keys to a Scion. Just like I wasn't about to ask him why he didn't also have work to get to.

Chevy opened my car door for me. I sat down and pressed the button on the side of the seat to move closer to the steering wheel. The seat slowly stuttered forward. Chevy had pushed it all the way back to accommodate his long legs. I, for the five thousandth time since I'd bought that Jetta, cursed whoever approved that feature instead of a manual slide that would have adjusted the seat in seconds.

"All right," he said once I was situated, then shut my car door.

On my drive home, the sun was still unbearable. I fished around in my armrest for a pair of sunglasses. With Chevy in my rearview, I thought ahead to the guy who'd texted me the night before and who I was sure I'd finally meet over the weekend.

I woke up that Sunday to a "good morning, beautiful" text. My date the night before had been a 6'6" amateur basketball player. He was so tall that even in heels, I had to raise my arm up like a little kid to hold his hand. His head dropped low at entryways; revolving doors made him claustrophobic. The fifteen inches between us meant that at the club, while we were dancing, he hadn't seen another man approach me, grab at my hips, and undulate his body against mine. My struggle to escape the stranger had knocked me backward, and I'd gripped my date's thighs to keep from falling. This had caused him to drop his gaze, see us, and shove the man off me.

After he'd watched the man retreat into the crowd, he'd leaned down, so I could hear him over the music, and said, "You're the type of pretty that's going to get me in trouble."

I'd looked at the razor-etched double notch in his eyebrow, the flames tattooed on his forearm, the italic script across his throat and doubted I was the one who was the trouble kind of pretty. (I was right. Things ended after he stole my phone and got another woman pregnant.)

During my morning pee, I blasted a post-date recap to my friends, texting with one hand and wiping with the other. Midwipe, I paused. There was something gooey down there, like a jellyfish had dropped dead between my thighs. I retrieved my hand. On my palm, nestled in a wad of toilet paper, was a used condom.

At 8:00 a.m., I was smelling latex. And me. And Chevy.

Chevy, who'd picked my drunk ass up from the bar on Thursday night. Thursday. It was Sunday. I was on a date with one guy while a condom from sex with another guy haunted my insides like Casper the Vaginal Canal Ghost. Sitting there in my little bathroom, with my underwear around my ankles, I didn't know you could feel that humiliated with no one around to bear witness to your embarrassment. I wanted to flush it and forget about it, but I had questions.

"YOU LEFT A FUCKING CONDOM INSIDE ME?" Sometimes, over text, tone can be unclear. This was not one of those times.

"I thought you knew. You went to the bathroom," Chevy texted back.

"TO PEE."

"I'm sorry, I really thought you knew. I told you I lost the condom."

This was a previously unexperienced consequence of drunk sex. Chevy and I weren't besties, but he knew me well enough to know that my response to "I lost the condom" would not have been to saunter off to pee, return moments later, and go directly to sleep. Hell no. I used a condom every. Single. Time. Especially with him, even though he frequently tried to convince me otherwise. "I lost the condom" is a series of words that would have made me leap right out of bed, pop a squat on his floor, and feverishly try to fish it out. There would be no sleep until the errant rubber was retrieved. My chill reaction should have been a signal to circle back to the topic in the morning.

"I had a date last night."

"I'm sorry."

What if I had brought my date home? I pictured the condom conga line that would have occurred inside me. Or worse, what if, like a foul magic trick, he sank into me wearing one condom and pulled out wearing two? What if the used condom had leaked out of me and onto the mattress like an afterbirth? How do you even explain something like that to someone?

More pressing than the what-ifs was that HIV stat blaring like a warning in the back of my mind. I couldn't trust Chevy to know his status or his girlfriend's status or the status of whoever she was doing her dirt with. My annual exam was a convenient time to get tested, but I only went every year because it was what I had to do to get a doctor to re-up my birth control prescription. So, if the average twentysomething dude never went to the doctor unless shit was dire—especially if he was unemployed and/or uninsured—I doubted he was going out of his way to get tested when plenty of them acted like putting on a condom was some great inconvenience.

Being the bedroom enforcer made me feel like a finger-wagging mom. "Eat your Wheaties; do your homework; wrap it up!" Why does it typically fall to women to act as safety patrol during hookups with men? Most of us sat in the same weak-ass, fear-based sex ed classes in high school. We'd seen the same slides of the worst-case scenarios of what could happen if we dared to embark on anything beyond abstinence. But if I didn't treat *condom* like the magic word that made sex suddenly appear—abracadabra!—most men were happy to act as if they didn't exist. Sometimes, it was a race to bring it up before a dude could slip his dick in me raw. This, obviously, was not OK. But the assumption that it was and the coercion I frequently experienced was consistent enough that it all just felt like a standard part of sleeping with men.

I sat on the toilet googling "early signs of HIV" so long that I had Gumby legs when I finally stood up. Essentially everything on the internet said the only way to know if you've got HIV is to get tested for HIV. I was still afraid of needles and still concerned about upholding a certain image with Dr. L. I was the type of person who used to shave before my annual exam but was careful to do it a week in advance so my hair could grow back just enough that it wouldn't look like I'd shaved specifically for the occasion. Needless to say, I was too embarrassed to return to Dr. L's office for the sole purpose of an HIV test. I did some research and found a drop-in clinic in Long Beach that administered an oral test.

The free clinic was in a trailer behind a shabby-looking hospital in a rundown part of Long Beach. I was a long way from Dr. L's cotton robes in Laguna Beach. "What will you do if your sample comes back positive for HIV?" asked Francisco, the counselor at the clinic.

I flipped the page in the open magazine on my lap to avoid his gaze. I'd thought a lot about that while waiting for my appointment. Ever the dramatic twentysomething, I told him, "Probably go home and kill myself."

This was more than a decade ago. I was ignorant about HIV/AIDS beyond what I'd seen in movies, which mostly revolved around gay white men. To me, it was little more than a sad plot point, the subtext of a TLC song, an urban legend about used needles left on movie theater seats. In the '90s, on TV, Black women who tested positive for HIV were using drugs or were the victims of Black men who were "on the down-low," fodder for daytime TV talk shows. It was sensationalist. It was homophobic. Biphobic. Transphobic. I did not see myself in those women. I was just a child watching whatever was on.

If I had not seen that tweet, my fear of contracting HIV would not have been immense enough to immediately go get tested. HIV was about as real to me as the boogeyman my mother told me lived in the sidewalk grates. I didn't believe her, but I walked around the grates, into the grass if I had to, just to be safe, just to be out of the reach of his grasp.

I continued to avoid Francisco's gaze. His office had a small window that looked out into a gravel parking lot. In the magazine, there was a coupon for fifty cents off a can of Campbell's chicken noodle soup. It'd expired two years earlier.

Francisco laid a hand on the magazine, preventing me from flipping the page. I made eye contact with him, then searched his tiny office for something else to look at. The space was cramped but organized. There was a stack of manila folders on his desk by a phone I knew was old because the last time they made things that shade of green was the '70s.

Only after I'd studied everything I possibly could did I return my gaze to Francisco. He was still looking at me, expecting me to say something more. I let loose a small sigh and hoped he didn't smell the Thai food I'd had for lunch on my breath. I shifted in my seat. My chair didn't get more comfortable. I listened to the fluorescent lights overhead until Francisco said to me, "You know, with the advancement in medications, HIV patients live full, unencumbered lives."

In college, one of my professors showed the HBO version of *Angels in America*. It was the first time I'd learned anything about the AIDS epidemic beyond a few passing mentions in textbooks. It was the first time I'd seen a story that treated people living with, dying from, and loving those with HIV/AIDS like actual people instead of like a cautionary tale. It wouldn't be until my thirties that I'd become friends with and know people who were openly living with HIV. Their lives were indeed full and—with reliable access to health care—unencumbered.

But back then, sitting in that tin-box clinic with Francisco, I knew no one. And truth be told, at the time, I was more worried about the stigma than I was about the health implications of a positive HIV test. Like having an abortion, acquiring HIV is treated as a moral failing. In the larger narrative of our society, AIDS is a gay man's punishment for being too free, and an unwanted pregnancy is a woman's.

Despite my belief that I should be allowed to do as I pleased with my body, including indulging in numerous sex partners, I could not entirely rid myself of the shame of sleeping around. The shame was like a hard popcorn kernel wedged between my back molars. Miniscule. Yet there was a painful awareness and an inability to dislodge it. To test positive for HIV would be confirmation that I was right to be ashamed about my sleeping around.

But by being uninformed about HIV and the realities of a life lived with HIV, I was contributing to the same stigma I feared. And that's the point of keeping someone ignorant and afraid. If I didn't know any better about my body and my health, I and it could be used by those who did. By a gyno doubling up my exams to spend more time with my breasts. By a conservative culture to uphold beliefs around who is good and clean and deserving of care in this country. As a Black woman,

I'd received the messaging—both directly and indirectly—that I was undeserving. And as a straight woman, that I was deserving only if I remained pure, the definition of which was ever shifting and unattainable. And if not pure, then I could at least evade judgment by maintaining the facade of respectability. Sitting in a free clinic waiting on an HIV test was at the expense of my respectability. Why did so much of what was necessary to care for my health threaten the facade? Birth control to manage my period. Requesting an STI screen to protect my partners and myself. Talking openly about the risk of HIV.

I know that there's no true safety in ignorance. It isn't bliss. Knowledge is power. But still, I struggled to drop the one shield I'd been given, the one form of supposed protection, to reach toward . . . What? I don't know. I was almost as afraid of the truth in knowing as I was of not knowing. Almost.

"Why are you here today?" Francisco asked me.

"A condom broke." I saw this more as a simplification of events than a lie.

He took out a yellow slip of paper. Printed on the paper was a questionnaire designed to calculate my HIV risk. I checked all of the "no" boxes. Again, he looked at me, then confirmed, "A condom broke? That's it?"

"Yeah . . . ?" I answered.

Francisco's surprise didn't make sense to me until deep into my thirties when I told this story to a group of friends. Although they knew the truth about the condom cocooned inside me for days, they, too, were surprised this particular incident led me to get tested. They wanted to know if I was really that afraid, if that level of fear was a realistic reaction. I repeated the statistic about Black women being the fastest-growing demographic of new HIV cases. They remained unswayed.

Here's the thing about getting your medical information off social media: sometimes, the information you need requires more context than a tweet can provide. Yes, it was true—the stat was backed by data from the CDC—that Black women made up the majority of new HIV cases among women in 2010 *and* that my fear was overblown. What was left unsaid in that tweet was that although Black women were the fastest-growing demographic among women, men still comprised the vast majority of HIV cases. That overall, HIV cases were dropping.

The CDC, Stanford Health, and various other sources clock my risk, as someone who has "vaginal receptive sex," of encountering HIV as less than 1 percent—or maybe not. The sites also note that stats can be unreliable; there are a myriad of variables that factor into your personal risk from any given sexual encounter. I'm a writer, not a doctor or a statistician. This isn't medical advice.

But still, no wonder Francisco was surprised by my visit.

I had expected to come to the free clinic, have my cheek swabbed, and sit out in the lobby reading old magazines until my results were ready. I hadn't come prepared to discuss next steps. I didn't want to leaf through pamphlets or contemplate the reality of living with HIV. But to Francisco—even though he was a bit baffled by my presence in his clinic—I was as worthy of an education as anyone else he met with. He didn't exploit my naiveté. He didn't cast judgment on the activities I might or might not have been participating in and, relatedly, what kind of person I was or wasn't based on those activities. He simply administered the test and provided relevant information.

Imagine if all care for my body was so straightforward.

If I was prescribed birth control for period pain—and received it. If I requested a breast exam—and it was given without commentary. If I said no to sex with a man—and he listened. If I said yes to sex with a man—and he put on a condom. If I asked if I should get an HIV test—and I was told what I needed to know to make an informed decision instead of ludicrous hypotheticals.

Fifteen minutes later, Francisco scooched his chair back from his desk and left the room to check on my sample. He returned with my results. The letters were large enough for me to read even before Francisco handed me the paper: *NEGATIVE.*

Chapter 11

CLICK

For my twenty-sixth birthday, I booked a night for me and my friends at a burlesque bar in LA. I wanted to do something classy. However, I drank as much as I would have at any of the Orange County dive bars we frequented, which led to me, by the end of the night, dripping drunk tears over a pair of $1.99 flip-flops. My feet don't tolerate high heels well, so I often kept a pair of flip-flops on me so I could switch midway through the night. In the car, ready for home, my friends refused to let me reenter the bar to retrieve my flip-flops, which they insisted I'd already placed in the trunk. This is how Henry's phone call found me.

Attempting to soothe me, he said, "Don't cry, darling. I love you." It was 2011, nearly two years after the first time he'd found me teary-eyed.

I hiccupped. "You, you love . . . me?"

"Of course I do."

I cried harder. I sobbed to my friend—who'd wisely taken my car keys and had slid into the driver's seat beside me—"Henry loves me!" My tears were so torrential, my false lashes fell from my lids. My next call was likely to Chevy, who'd never confessed his love for me but who'd absolutely be down to deliver on some birthday sex.

Henry and I had resided in a romantic negative space for years, but now that he'd verbally confirmed he loved me, I felt emboldened. Later that week, sober, I texted him, pressing him for more out of our relationship. He held steady. His jokey flirtations didn't appease me.

Later, I saw he'd tweeted, "We can't go back, and we can't go forward, but is where we're at so bad?"

I immediately pictured us on a seesaw, suspended forever midmotion. I tweeted back, "Yes."

Henry melted down. He tweeted about previous relationships. Not everything he said made sense. There were so many fragments. His secrets were riddled with more secrets. I watched from afar, then eased off Twitter. We stopped speaking.

Shortly after, I moved to LA for my new job. One day, I received a message from Henry on LinkedIn. His employer had messed up his paperwork. He couldn't stay in the States. He wanted to see me before he returned to Nigeria.

It would not have been unreasonable for me to tell Henry no. We hadn't had an honest conversation about anything that had happened between us. I wasn't interested in reprising my role in our sitcom romance for one final, very special episode. But this was the boy who hadn't left me crying in a bar, who'd taken me to see fireworks after that terrifying afternoon with a marine, and who popped up in the middle of my bad dates to steal me away for ice cream. How could I refuse him during his own moment of heartbreak? Although my life had moved forward from him—I lived in a new city! I had a new job! I never went to Sharkeez anymore!—my heart had not. One brief LinkedIn message, and I was floating toward Henry again.

I drove down to Orange County to see him. When I arrived at his apartment complex, I slid my debit card into the reader, the gate opened, and down came Henry, fully clothed. He brought out a vintage camera and would periodically raise it to snap a picture of me. Over ice cream–filled mochi. Click. By the firepit at the Orange County Mining

Company, the view overlooking all of Orange County. Click. At his apartment, his captain's hat cocked on my head. Click. Arm around me, kissing me, kissing me, kissing me. Click. Click. Click. Finally.

At the end of the night, Henry walked me out to my car, down several sets of steps, and across multiple now-familiar walkways. I no longer had my Jetta or kept a fat binder of CDs in my car, but how I felt about Henry had not changed. I turned to him. "Let's go to Vegas. Right now. You don't have to leave. I'd do that for you." Marry a man who'd only ever kissed me twice—the first night we met and our last night together—and nothing more? I'd never made a more romantic proposition in my life. Perhaps, I hadn't completely lost the Harlequin plot on love.

Henry laughed, mouth wide, head back. "Aw, honey, there are far wealthier women than you I could marry." He was teasing. I knew he wouldn't be marrying any of those women, either. So much had changed between us, and yet nothing at all had changed between us. What is the end-of-the-story equivalent of a meet-cute? This was Henry's and mine.

On the drive home, my car smelled of Van Cleef & Arpels. I wasn't sure that I'd ever see Henry again. Next to me, on the passenger's seat, his captain's hat rode alongside me back to LA, back to my life without him. And it came with me to every city I lived in after that—hanging off a door in my bedroom, sometimes perched atop my bookshelf—hoping someday to be reunited with its owner, like a crown returning to its rightful heir.

Years into the future, Henry will call me on my birthday from wherever he's living in the world and again on Valentine's Day, just as he has every year since he left Southern California. I will have moved home to Louisville. My cousin will sit in my home sipping tea and tell me about their partner. My cousin will describe it as a romantic-platonic relationship. I will not believe them. I will think of them and their partner as two people afraid to reveal their true emotions—that this cannot last. That they will need to go back to just friends or move forward to what I deem is a *real relationship*. To what I've been told is a real relationship. Midmotion seesaws must fall or rise eventually.

I will believe this despite still being single—despite learning to let Harlequin plots go almost entirely. When my cousin talks about something their partner has done, I will give them a knowing look. When I see their booed-up photos on Instagram, I will quadruple tap, as if the additional intensity will be evident in my digital like.

I will watch my cousin and their partner date other people. I will watch those other people break their hearts. I will watch them put each other back together. I will wait for them to become "more." But in the future, it's me who will change, not them.

On a birthday call with Henry, I will ask him, "What if the language had existed for what we were?" I will wonder aloud if we would have caused each other so much confusion and frustration, if I still would have grappled for more, if he would have continued to be so insistent about offering less.

"You're right, honey," he will say with the kind of happy-sad that says we can't go back, and we can't move forward. But at least I will know where we are isn't so bad.

I will see that I can continue to feel entitled to the narrow Harlequin-brand love that life has denied me, that has never fulfilled me even when I've managed to find it, or I can choose to become expansive. I can admit that the love I receive will not always come to me as the love I thought I wanted—but that will make it no less worthy of a place in my life. And maybe that paint-by-numbers, prescriptive kind of love isn't the kind I want any longer—just as little else I wanted at twelve is what I still want in my thirties. Or, possibly, have ever wanted.

Chapter 12

THE HOLY GRAIL

Tanya, Jessica, and I arrived at the Cicada Club in downtown LA just after sunset. The art deco entryway was tiled in white marble with a gold-frame design. Glowing columns trimmed in more gold stood at each side of the double doors. The ceiling was inset with large slices of angled, lit glass that gave the effect of standing beneath an upturned candy dish. And we were the sweets.

We were at the Cicada Club for the Urban League's 2011 Black History Month Mixer. When we joined the Urban League, we'd told ourselves it was to network with other Black professionals. We said that our involvement on committees would look good on our résumés. We wanted to give back to the community, we insisted. But what we really wanted was to meet men. Black men. More specifically, Black men with degrees and careers that matched our own. We soon found out that we weren't alone. At every meeting, there were at least three women for every man, a ratio that worsened when you subtracted the men with visible wedding bands. But after months of meetings and mixers, my friends and I had arrived in downtown Los Angeles with renewed hope. The Urban League was hosting the mixer with several other organizations popular with LA's Black and bougie crowd. Perhaps the male-to-female ratio would be more in our favor.

We had heard the stories in the news—that the ratio would *never* be in our favor, that we had more education and earned more than our male counterparts. But those stories only made us strive harder for the unachievable. We were women, after all, accustomed to being the exception. We were not there to settle; we were on a quest for the holy grail of men.

I was wearing a red dress with a collar that draped over my shoulder; a double line of buttons marched down my chest. I felt very Jackie O. After the mixer, I had dinner lined up with a musician. A date I'd only agreed to because the mixer meant I was already making the drive from Orange County to LA, as I hadn't moved there yet. The musician was in town on business with his band. Each member had a signature color, and they exclusively dressed in it from head to toe—like a roving pack of crayons. It hadn't occurred to me that the two of us dressed in red and green would look like Christmas décor.

I was attracted to Green. He had that lead-singer charisma all front men have. When we met in Austin, he'd pleaded for a date—following me around the SXSW trade show floor with his Crayola crew until I agreed. Then, he'd stood me up. He spent the next year texting me regularly and inviting me to visit him in DC. "I'll pay for the ticket," he offered each time. I could imagine standing on the arrivals curb with my luggage for at least an hour before he finally texted to tell me he wasn't coming. *Something came up,* he'd say.

Even as I looked forward to our date, I wasn't certain that Green deserved a second chance. Still, it was exciting, for once, to be pursued by an artist whose creative endeavors were paying off. But aside from his flakiness, I had other concerns. Green never called me, nor did he put energy into getting to know me better. Just the texts pleading with me to visit. He was showing me interest without showing interest *in* me. Maybe he didn't want a relationship with me for real, but I was not about to endure the six-hour flight to DC for a hookup. I could easily hook up with men in my own time zone. I was not Ludacris; I did not need hoes in every area code.

Inside the Cicada Club, the dining room was empty. The plush red carpet silenced the click-click of our heels. Polished wood posts shone in the light of a large crystal chandelier. The tables were dressed in crisp white linen and unlit tea lights. There was the anticipation of things to come. The work-dinner scene in *Pretty Woman* was shot in that dining room, the one where Julia Roberts sends a piece of escargot flying. The name of the restaurant had changed, and the furniture had been replaced, but monied elegance was still the ambiance.

As we walked up the stairs to the mezzanine, Tanya told me, "They have swing dancing here on the weekends. They move the tables aside and lay down a dance floor." I envisioned the Cicada Club at the height of its art deco glory, the women in fringe dresses and headbands decorated with gems and feathers and the men dressed in tuxes—the kind they rarely wore anymore, not even to their own weddings. I could almost hear the big band, the thrum of the stand-up bass, the hoot of the horns.

We paid our cover, then entered the private event. There were a few other people in the room, but it was clear, by the mellow jams the DJ was spinning, that we were early. There was a scattering of small tables on one end, a dance floor on the other, and a spread of appetizers against the far wall.

As the room began to fill, the crowd skewed older than we had hoped, but there were a few prospects. A light-skinned man in a camel blazer approached us. He was in law school. Jessica angled her body toward him. She was interested. She began her interview-style line of questioning: "Which law school? Where do you work? Where are you from?" Tanya and I did what we could to make the interaction an actual conversation.

The man stood with us long enough for his cocktail napkin to go dark with condensation. He used a skinny red straw to flick the ice cubes around in his glass, and then, after thirty minutes of chatting and flirting, he said it: "My fiancée . . ."

DISENGAGE. DISENGAGE. DISENGAGE. Jessica, Tanya, and I veered away in haste, barely allowing him to complete his sentence.

"He did that on purpose. He wanted the attention. Should have mentioned her sooner," Jessica huffed, holding her glass tight and looking around the room for another man. We were on a quest. We did not have time to waste, not even ten minutes, on the wrong guy when faced with such a competitive dating terrain.

Most of the men who approached us were too young or too old. The only one who gave me any real attention was in his late fifties, dressed in an outdated, ill-fitting suit, and he had a Jheri curl. He closed in on me while I was over by the appetizers, balancing a petite plate and my drink in one hand and using my other hand for the platter tongs. "Excuse me," I said as I navigated around him and toward the safety of my friends. The array of men at the mixer made me happy I'd decided to give Green another chance.

Green had meetings all day but said he'd call me at 7:00 p.m. to figure out dinner. Seven o'clock ticked along to seven thirty, and Green still had not called me. I stepped out of the mixer to call him. I was more than ready to leave. The dining room had filled. The noise of the patrons carried up to the mezzanine. When he said hello, I plugged an ear with my finger so I could hear Green better. I could also hear the voices of everyone else around him better.

"Hey, you were supposed to call me about dinner."

"Oh, we're already at dinner. Roscoe's. A group thing."

"I like Roscoe's."

"I didn't even think to invite you."

"How could you not think to invite me to dinner when we already had dinner plans?"

"We'll get together tomorrow."

Again, he blew me off with such ease, as if he hadn't been the one pursuing me for over a year. I guess I should have been thankful he answered his phone instead of texting me hours later.

In Austin, when we met, I remembered texting him and receiving no answer. I'd walked around downtown under the setting sun, killing time, trying to wait for a response from him even though my feet ached from hours of standing on the convention floor. I remembered how I was sitting alone at a table next to a pair on a first date when Green finally texted to tell me he couldn't make it: "Something came up." I remembered it so well, I wasn't sure why I was allowing him to drag me through a repeat experience.

I was tired of this behavior from men. What joy did they derive from being repeatedly disappointing? Why is it that if you give a man a second chance, he will disappoint you in the exact same way he disappointed you the first time? Not even in a new and exciting way, but the exact same fuckup. For a year, Green had gotten to play at being sorry and lob his best charm offensive at me, but when it was time for words to become actions, for things to get real in LA, he was like Pinocchio telling Jiminy Cricket, *Never mind, I'll stay a marionette.*

Before abruptly hanging up on Green, I made it clear that there would be no tomorrow. He didn't call me back. I wasn't sure whether to be more or less angry about that. Either he was being respectful, or he'd simply gone right back to enjoying his dinner—without me.

Back at the mixer, the DJ in the corner was working his way through Top 40 tracks, and the energy in the room was rising. Tanya and Jessica were chatting with two men, but Tanya's dry smile and Jessica's eyes—continuously sailing over and around them—told me these men didn't have a chance. One of the men was shorter, rounder, and lighter. He had freckles. There were shades of red in the beard that sprouted, full and bushy, at his jawline. His smile was big and genuine, his face overly animated in his attempt to maintain my friends' attention. The other man was a thinner, darker, younger guy with locs dangling down his back. He was quiet, letting his friend take the lead. A wooden rosary hung around his neck and rested against the purple button-down shirt he'd layered under a black jacket. His eyebrows, goatee, and mustache looked as if an artist had drawn his facial hair on with a series of fine, wispy strokes. As I joined the group, I looked down at his skateboard shoes. I was feeling feisty after my call with Green, so I asked him, "Who wears Nike Dunk Lows to a networking event?"

He gave my look right back to me. "Who wears fishnets to a networking event?"

"These are not fishnets. They're patterned stockings," I said of my black netted paisley-*patterned* hosiery.

"I see," he said. "I'm Hunter."

The DJ threw on "Cupid Shuffle." Our friends, and most everyone else, headed for the dance floor. The two of us were left talking. Well, us and the Jheri curl guy from earlier. He was hovering nearby. Hunter looked over his shoulder at the man, then moved slightly into Jheri curl guy's view of me.

"I'm Minda." I handed him a business card.

"Is this your real phone number, Minda?" My grin was my answer. "I want your real number," he said.

The Jheri curl guy came in closer, like he was getting impatient for his turn to talk to me. Again, Hunter moved into his line of sight. "What is up with this creeper?" he asked me. "Is he for real right now?"

"He's been doing this all night."

I looked at Hunter, and I wanted to feel the heft of his hair in my hand. I gave him my real number.

He told me he was from DC, but he'd been in LA all month. "Can I take you to brunch on Saturday?" he asked. What were the odds of getting stood up by one DC guy, only to be asked out by another? He'd attended Florida A&M University and had a degree in marketing but primarily earned his income DJing. Degree and a career. College educated and creative. We'd have as much fun at a professional networking event as we would at a show for an underground rapper. I could see he cared about his appearance without being overly into designer labels. But most importantly, he asked me out within minutes of meeting me, versus some men who'd take my number and then text for so many weeks without setting a plan that I'd begin to wonder whether they wanted a date or a pen pal. For the first time ever at an Urban League event, I'd met exactly the type of man I'd been searching for. I had found my holy grail.

The event photographer weaving through the crowd stopped in front of us. He motioned with his camera that he'd like to take a picture and waved for Hunter to put his arm around my shoulder. When the photographer gave us a preview of the photo, I saw that I had reflexively tilted my head toward Hunter's.

On Saturday morning, I was wrapped in a towel, skin still damp from the shower, when my phone rang. It was Hunter. "I'm really sorry. This thing came up, and my friend needs me to go with him to take footage. Can we do dinner tomorrow night instead?"

I'd been there before. Guy cancels last minute, reschedules, and then is never heard from again. Or worse, it's just an endless cycle of canceled plans and makeup plans, like with Green. Standing in front of my bathroom mirror, I decided not to let my bad feelings over Green shade what could be with Hunter. "Yeah, OK, tomorrow."

On Sunday, I woke up feeling confident that the date wasn't happening. I didn't want to spend a ton of time getting ready, only to learn I had nowhere to go. I waited until the very last minute to slip on my dress and do my makeup. Drawing on eyeliner, I thought about how it would sting if he canceled and how I'd have to relive the embarrassment with each friend who asked me about my date the next day. Relief would ride just beneath some of their tones of sympathy while I told them the date hadn't happened. Relief that another woman in their social circle had not pulled ahead of them in the race for the ring. We shared the subtle fear that all of our friends were just one good date away from retiring from the go-to ladies' night we faced each weekend. Our goal was not so much about being married as it was about not being the *last* to be married.

As I stood at the mirror, passing my flat iron through my hair, a text from Hunter pinged on my phone, asking me if I liked sushi, which was followed by another text with an address to a restaurant in Silver Lake. Someone knew how to keep a dinner date. I climbed out of the bog of pessimism I'd been wallowing in and headed out the door.

In Silver Lake, I parked in the lot behind the sushi spot. As I was walking around to the front of the restaurant, I was washed in the light of a car inching its nose into the alley. I stepped onto the curb in front of the entrance. The car stopped, and Hunter exited from the passenger side. The energy that welled up inside me when I saw him wasn't first-date jitters; it felt more like the excitement of seeing a lover who'd returned from a long trip. We had been reunited.

The sushi restaurant was nothing fancy, but it was clean, and the yellow walls and blond hardwood floors gave it warmth. A chef in a white paper hat was bent over his work behind the sushi bar. There was a silver-haired couple cuddled up at the back corner table.

We had so much to talk about, we kept forgetting to look at the menu. Each time the server checked in, we made another attempt to choose a few rolls, but then we'd start in again on another topic. He told me about DC. I told him about Louisville. He told me about going to school at an HBCU, and I told him about the unbearable whiteness of being in Orange County. Each time the server returned to our table, we were again reminded we were there to have a meal. Finally, we chose two rolls and then took more than two hours to eat them. I could have sat there all night if it didn't mean keeping the restaurant staff there all night, too. The chill in the server's voice each time she passed by and we told her we were "good for now" did nothing to cool our mood.

It was the way he looked at me that made me wish our date would never end. It was as if he was holding me in place and time with his eyes, like I knew I existed only because he saw me. And he really saw me. I'd been on dates with men whose eyes told me their ears weren't listening to a word I was saying; they were probably too busy plotting how to get me home. But in Hunter's eyes, I could see he was carefully taking in each word.

"They are really going at it!" I said about the grandparents in the corner. Their hands were finding their way into private places in a public space.

Hunter turned around to get a look. His head quickly snapped back. "Oh, wow."

Their hot-and-heaviness—right in my eyeline—was a constant reminder that we were on a first date, a date that might or might not end with a kiss. I wanted it to end with a kiss. I wanted him to want it to end with a kiss.

"When do you go back to DC?" I asked.

"Tomorrow."

Tomorrow. I felt like Indiana Jones in *The Last Crusade*, fingers stretched out to save the Holy Grail from tumbling down into an endless abyss. Here he was. The man I'd been searching for, and tomorrow he'd be on the other side of the country. One night was not enough time. What was the point of meeting him, only to be swiftly ripped apart again?

I offered to give him a ride home so his friend didn't have to pick him up. He followed me down the alley and opened my door for me. It might seem like it'd be awkward to have a guy open the door for you when you're the one doing the driving, but it was cute. Inside the car, I queued up an up-and-coming rapper out of Mississippi to flex my tastes in music a bit. I wanted to impress this DJ.

"K.R.I.T.'s got another mixtape dropping next month," he said, recognizing the artist.

"I know—I can't wait."

I was disappointed to find that when he'd said his friend lived a few minutes from the restaurant, he was being literal. Less than five turns and we were there. It was time to say goodbye, and I was not ready to let go of the night. I pulled into the parking lot that stretched across the front of the apartment building and put my car in park. We both sat very still.

"Thanks again for dinner," I said and courageously turned my head so I could look into his eyes.

He waited a beat, then said, "You're welcome. Let me know if you ever make it out to DC." He unbuckled his seat belt. Instead of reaching for me as I had hoped, he reached for the door handle. That was it, the end of our date. Before pulling off, I watched him until he disappeared into one of the apartments on the second floor. One last glint of my holy grail before he was gone for good.

A few months later, I started the new job that moved me up to LA. The company flew me out to DC for training and a conference. The luck! I saw Hunter again. We argued over who was going to pay for dinner until I insisted it was my company, not me, picking up the bill. We went to a blues bar, Madam's Organ, where our bodies stood close together on crowded stairs. He drove me around the city, showing me his DC, a DC that had gentrified drastically over the years.

That trip was my first time in the capital. Earlier in the day, the city had frustrated me, each intersection a multitude of streets crisscrossing at every angle. With a conference to work, there'd been no time to see the monuments and the museums. But seated in Hunter's car, looking out on the personal landmarks of a life lived revealed the real reason the universe had seen fit to align our stars once again: I was there to fall in love. This time, the evening ended with a kiss. And more.

We attempted to stay in touch, but we lived on separate coasts. Our check-ins became less frequent. When he moved to New York City, I made a trip out there under the only-slightly-true premise of visiting friends. He took me to see a glass-encased carousel, then snapped my photo by the Brooklyn waterfront in DUMBO. We went out with his friends one night, and each one was just as kind as he was. Any stray moment at the bar that found me without him, a friend would, unprompted, assure me that Hunter was all that he seemed to be.

Back on the West Coast, I continued to date, continued to be disappointed by men. Hunter had a lot of ambition. I knew he was focused on achievement—the type of man whose main motivator in life is to buy his hardworking mama a home—and wasn't ready for a serious relationship, much less a cross-coast, long-distance love affair. Still, every time I saw him, it was a confirmation that exactly what I wanted in a man did exist.

We weren't serious, but he took me seriously. He was caring and sensitive. Whenever I was with him, I knew I mattered. When reflecting on my dating choices, I held Hunter on one side and any potential love interest on the other, like a relationship-themed *Goofus and Gallant*. It wasn't hard to see who was Gallant and who was a doofus. Hunter was proof I didn't have to settle for yo-yo boys like Green. That I wasn't asking for too much. That it was possible to keep a relationship casual and be kind.

Years after I met Hunter, while I was nursing a broken heart in grad school, he happened to come through Riverside on a tour. He stayed with me. Did my dishes (and my roommates' dishes) and cleaned my room while I was in class. He had gone to work by the time I got home but left a small gift and a sweet note on my pillow. The next night, I made him dinner, he came to a play put on by one of the other writers in my cohort, and I drove out to Santa Monica with him for a DJ gig. I ended the night on the dance floor, sweaty and red-cheeked, his hat on my head. Smiling. He was easy to be with.

That may not seem like much, but chaos sprouted wild and plentiful while dating in my twenties and well into my thirties . . . Sometimes, it was chaos I sowed by not being direct, by not speaking up, by not asking the necessary questions. And some of it was chaos brought to me by men who, when confronted with my directness, were dishonest, evasive, and withholding. Both scenarios left me distraught and emotionally spun out. So, for a man to be exactly who he presented himself as was refreshing—here for the moment with no illusions about the future, a true friendship at the core of our connection. Hunter wasn't a puzzle for me to solve. He was a person who wanted to know and be known by me. And what I had with him didn't have to grow into anything more than it was for me to appreciate it.

Five years after meeting Hunter, I moved back home to Louisville. He reached out to say a tour was taking him through Lexington: How far was that from me? Was it too short notice? Too long a drive for dinner that night? Just as I had for our first date, I made the drive to a city slightly more than an hour from me to see him. But this time, I didn't hesitate as I dressed and did my makeup. Again, we had sushi. Again, he opened my door even though I was driving. And again, I hoped he might kiss me, and he didn't. I wasn't disappointed, though.

On our first date, when Hunter told me he was leaving the next day, I'd felt like Indiana Jones. But I hadn't actually seen *Indiana Jones and the Last Crusade* since the '90s. I recently returned to the scene where the ground splits open, and it was as I remembered—Indy's fingers wriggling, the grail so close. But I'd forgotten that just before he finds himself over the edge, he first tries to save a woman in the same predicament. She's certain she can grab the grail. One hand in his, the other grasping at the gold chalice. He begs her to hold on to him with both hands so he can pull her to safety. She doesn't. Down into the abyss she goes. Then, Indy is over the edge, his father's grip around his hand slipping and Indy reaching, reaching for the grail. His father calmly says his name, and Indiana looks at him and knows the grail ain't worth dying over. He places both hands over his father's and is saved. Knowing the grail exists, drinking from it, and being restored by it would have to be enough. Distance and timing meant the same for Hunter and me.

If I'd expected our connection to hold all of my relationship hopes and wants, it would have pulled me over the edge. I wasn't meant to future-trip on what we could be, just experience what we were.

By the time I saw Hunter in Lexington, I already understood my holy grail wasn't my happily ever after. Just a sweet reminder that love could be both mythical and real. On the drive home, when the station I was listening to went staticky, I switched the radio off and let the night tell me stories about where I was headed as it whooshed past my open window.

Chapter 13

Viagra Falls

For years, birthdays meant drunk sex with Chevy—*orgasm, whisk me away!*—my night ending cradled in blackout sleep. For the last three Januaries, I'd woken up to a new year, tangled in bed with my old problems. But 2012 was different. Mainly, because Chevy wasn't fucking any sad girls. "Twenty-seven is so oooooold!" I sobbed into his bare chest.

"It's not any fun if you're crying, Minda," Chevy tucked away his dick, then rolled off me. A fuckboy with ethics.

I'd just turned an age in that middle ground between two milestones: college graduation and turning thirty. To me, thirty was this unspoken deadline to have every "adulthood" box checked: Career. Marriage. Homeownership. Kids. The default American dream. A measuring stick for the masses. My parents had three kids and a house in the 'burbs by the latter half of their twenties. The girls I'd gone to high school with back in Louisville had checked those adulthood boxes ages ago. They were all grown-for-real, complaining about their mortgages and their nipples, cracked from breastfeeding. Meanwhile, in SoCal, my late twenties weren't looking much different from my early twenties. Every weekend still played out like a Gucci Mane hook—*"Party, party, party! Let's all get wasted."* Cîroc stains on my fourteen-dollar bodycon dresses. Swapping texts and sometimes more with guys whose names weren't worth remembering at the time, much less now. And I hadn't heard a single tick or tock from my biological clock—babies could wait. Indefinitely.

I wasn't a total failure-to-launch case. I did have a decent sales job—scratch that, *career*—even if selling automatic faucets wasn't necessarily my life's dream. However, Forever 21 and LA rental rates were conspiring against my finances. Despite my corporate card and the company car, I was nowhere near homeownership. I'd moved from Orange County up to LA for that career. My two-bedroom, two-bath apartment with tandem parking in Silver Lake had come with a roommate who liked to date the most questionable dudes. But who was I to judge?

I jerked the sheets back from Chevy and kept crying until the vodka in my system ushered me to sleep, unassisted by birthday sex.

In the morning, I peered over Chevy's shoulder at the dusty GRE study guide on my desk, the stack of unopened credit card statements on my bedside, and the discarded price tags that speckled my floor like oversize confetti. Seeing the mess all around me, I vowed it was time to clean up my life. To paraphrase Prince, *Two thousand twelve: Party's over. Oops, out of time.*

But where to start? Apply to grad schools? Wrangle my spending? Roll a fuckboy outta my bed? Why not go about changing my circumstances by focusing completely on the one thing that wasn't within my realm of control: everlasting love.

I was on some avoidant bullshit, for sure, but I also had a need to begin with the biggest challenge. I distilled getting into grad school down to doing the paperwork, opening that GRE book, staring at the pages, and thinking about their contents really hard. Saving money wasn't much more than cooking the food in my fridge—instead of letting it rot—and no more payday pilgrimages to the mall. I'd already gotten into college once and had, at one point, maintained a cushy savings account. These were things I knew I could do. But love? Well, love required the cooperation of a second party. It meant no more on-again, off-again light-switch romances. I needed to find a man who wanted to be by my side when I blew out the candles on my birthday cake at the beginning of the night, not just pop up at the end after I'd drank enough to blow an alarming number on a BAC test. But Chevy, and the various iterations of him I'd dated over the last several years, had left me uncertain about my ability to pull off a long-term partnership.

I'd also tried to conquer love first because a relationship is the cheat code to making everything else easier. If you're middle class, you get a pass on the other adulthood must-haves if you appear to be in a healthy, functioning, heteronormative marriage. And dual incomes make home-ownership and child-rearing more achievable, especially when gender pay inequality denies women the full value of our labor. Besides, a relationship was the thing that I and most Black women I knew were missing from our lives, despite our many successes. Even those of us with fully decorated homes, hard-earned careers, and robust savings accounts capable of funding regular and consistent international travel. As a role model, we had power lawyer and mother to Black excellence in the making, Michelle LaVaughn Robinson Obama, in the White House with her adoring husband, and still, dating was just harder for us than the white girls.

The statistics say we're half as likely to be married. Blame it on mass incarceration. Blame it on the education gap. Blame it on poverty. But generally, it's Black women who'll be blamed for why we're still alone. Standards too high. Standards too low. When it comes to love, Black women don't get to have any standards—or be the standard, either.

For me, adulthood wasn't a threshold worth venturing past unpart-nered. Single women aren't taken seriously. Men are allowed to live their fullest lives *before* settling down, but a woman's life doesn't begin *until* she settles down. A woman who's made it to any notable point without finding a husband along the way has made a mistake. She's sure to be depicted as the bitter, demanding executive with an assistant slyly plotting to get their boss laid so they don't have to endure any more workplace abuse. Dating. Wedding planning. Marriage. Keeping house. All schemes to monopolize straight women's time. Not that we have much of it left after counting calories and perfecting no-makeup makeup looks, which we apparently do to impress each other and not men. Suuuuuure. Our beauty, our intellect, our worthiness to pass on our DNA are upheld by one metric: *Does a man want to commit to me for forever?*

Here's the thing. If you want to be Miss Independent, you can march right on into the Land of Grown-Ups all by yourself. You go on ahead and show the world it's wrong about your worth, but everyone else will be too busy holding hands with their soulmate to applaud for you. I had to know, even then, that the system was rigged against me, but I couldn't shake the belief that I would never gain a certain level of comfort and confidence in my life choices until I had someone to come home to. I needed a man who looked at me with such deep adoration at the end of every workday that I no longer worried about whether I should be contributing more to my 401(k). A man who got so caught up in our plans for the weekend, it didn't matter that my plans for my future felt like a dream I was struggling to remember several hours after waking up. I clung to the idea that being loved as is by someone could hush the turmoil of who and what I should be and when I should be it by. I didn't even notice I was reconstructing the same mousetrap I'd out-maneuvered at twenty-three when I broke up with Tyler. The wrong life for me then, now new and improved with the right man, the right job, and the right place to live. Because what other life did I know to pursue?

If I wanted to be married by thirty, I needed to meet a man imme-diately. Well, maybe not immediately. The morning after my birthday, I caressed Chevy's shoulder and asked tear-free, "Morning sex?"

Five months later, it was May, and I'd made little progress toward finding a boyfriend (or making any other major improvements). I hadn't yet learned that expecting your life to change without first changing yourself is kinda ineffective. So, I headed out on yet another first date.

The last dude had shown up in a dingy black hoodie that smelled like he'd spent his laundry coins on kush instead. The whole date, he'd complained about his Persian ex-girlfriend's racist family and shared stories about his childhood invisible friend between long jags of scrolling through his phone. When I suddenly stood to leave, he put some bass in his voice and demanded I sit back down. I didn't.

It was a time before Tinder. A time before Bumble. A time before Hinge. We were in the pre-swipe-apps-that-lead-to-quickie-connections era. Each bad date was more than one night wasted. In the lead-up, I'd spent serious time with my laptop on actual dating websites creating full profiles with multiple paragraphs about my hobbies, interests, personality, and what I wanted in a partner—crafted to hit that perfect blend of desirable without being intimidating—and patiently exchanging enough messages to confirm dude wasn't going to be the reason I turned up missing. I'd logged too many hours online just to meet a guy and get a contact high off his wardrobe. All while my GRE study guide continued to collect dust. I wasn't reading. I wasn't writing. I'm pressed to even think of a TV show I'd watched that year.

When I first began online dating, the digital magic of the internet offered up an alternative to men at bars who placed unwanted hands on my hips and ass, attempting to get my attention and my number. Online, I had more than a face and a few slick lines to go off to decide whether we were a match. Now, dating apps have re-created the bar experience on our smartphones. But even before I could swipe through a hundred profiles in less than an hour to confirm that every man in my vicinity was not the man for me, I'd begun to lose hope in the online-dating process. None of the sites had led me to anyone substantial.

Match.com was expensive and branded like business-casual dating. eHarmony was a youth pastor convincing you Christ was cool on the low. I mainly used OkCupid with its cute-nerdy vibe. Back then, OkCupid liked to tell people how long you'd been on their site. It made me feel like guys would see that I'd been a member for years and treat me like a carton of eggs weeks past its sell-by date—*prolly still good, but worth the risk?* I've heard that every year removed a woman is from twenty-two, the number of messages she receives drops drastically.

Plenty of Fish was also free, so I used it, too—even though its web design made it look like Craigslist's little cousin. And Plenty of Fish is where I met Keon.

For our first date, Keon chose a high-end Mexican spot on the early wave of charging for chips and "flights of salsa." It's the kind of place you'll find in any gentrified neighborhood, right next to the Pilates studio and just past the ukulele shop. Welcome to Silver Lake. I lived right around the corner.

Keon stood outside the restaurant, wearing the same black slim-cut Levi's and white thermal from his profile pic. He even had the same top two buttons undone. His baby 'fro tidy, his square-framed black glasses smudge-free. He watched as I strutted across Sunset Boulevard like a magnificent fucking unicorn. The My Little Pony of magnificent fucking unicorns. Glowing and glorious. Strong and proud in my eight-inch wedges. Clop, clop. My hair rippled down my back in bourbon waves. Car headlights racing forward in the night served as my personal spotlight. I was first-date ready.

We did that whole awkward hug-handshake-hug greeting, our arms and hands attempting to articulate, *Hi. Hello. Yes. I don't know you. But I want to know you! But I don't know you right now.* We settled on a hug, and then the hostess led us to the patio, where several other couples were already sharing dishes of sizzling fajitas, burritos coated in mole sauce, and corn drizzled with crema. I slipped into a chair beneath lanterns that crisscrossed high above our heads, their bellies glowing red, yellow, green, and blue. The table was so small, my wedges bumped up against his Chucks.

He'd told me he was a grad student, which meant free chips should have been a prerequisite for any restaurant he chose. I looked at the menu and then, out of concern for his budget, suggested, "Let's just split an app and some tacos. I'm not very hungry."

He was quick to agree. "Yeah, let's do that."

"But I'm going to need my own drink," I teased.

I didn't feel shy at all when he looked at me. I held his gaze, and he held mine, matching sets of brown eyes. He was from the East Coast, in LA getting his PhD in African American literature. His focus: Baldwin.

Over tacos, we talked books, our fingers pinched together around small corn tortillas. After a sip from his mezcal cocktail, he said, almost conspiratorially, "I have the biggest crush on Toni Morrison," and my heart flickered.

The list of men I'd dated who'd heard of Toni Morrison, much less had read any of her books, was tragically short. I thought dating this man might bring me back to the things I loved, like books and writing, possibly even motivate me about grad school. It can be easy to think you're falling in love with someone when really, you're falling for the glimmers of your possible self you see in them. A unique kind of narcissism. Many years later, when I took on the title of professor myself, I was the one who was most surprised. And yet, somehow, I saw this man, who was already progressing toward what I hadn't known I aspired to, as my equal. And why wouldn't I? There's a greater cultural obligation for me, as a woman, to find a man with potential than to fulfill my own.

Later that night, when I let him kiss me, Keon's fingers rested against my spine like I was the book he wanted to love next.

The following weekend, Keon asked me on a second date. He'd suggested dancing (even though his vibe was more chill lounge guy). "But you pick the bar," he said over the phone. "I'm still not really sure where to go in LA."

Downtown LA was desolate after dark, but Broadway Bar had a solid crowd that night. The décor was dark and moody; booths and velvet sofas and chairs in deep-red upholstery lined the walls. A massive, dimly lit chandelier hung over a circular bar where four bartenders scurried around, filling drinks. I'd been to that bar enough times that friends had begun to associate me with it. They would post about it on my Facebook wall whenever they recognized it on TV or in a movie masquerading as some fictional place.

As body temperatures rose on the small dance floor, the smells of perfumes, deodorants, hair products, and BO all comingled. Keon and I were at the center, with the crowd crushing in on us from all directions, pushing us closer and closer together. The DJ controlled us like a puppet master, throwing on a fast song to work the crowd into a frenzy or a slow jam to bring us back down again.

On our first date, Keon and I never stopped talking. On our second date, few words were spoken, but just as much was said. I felt sweaty and sexy. Keon was feeling it, too; he was not at all bashful about where he put his hands.

The DJ slipped into a '90s R&B set. *"At night I think of you, I want to be your lady, baby . . ."* Keon pulled my hips into his and tipped his face downward.

"Every night I pray I can call you my man . . ." I hooked my fingers in the loops of his black Levi's and tipped my face upward.

He moved in to kiss me. I pressed my face into the kiss, knocking his glasses askew.

Keon's kiss was confident without being aggressive; his teeth didn't forcefully knock into my teeth. His lips rested warmly against my lips, and his tongue nudged my tongue gently—an invitation. Intermittently, I'd break our kiss, but we'd barely make it to the next song before his mouth returned to my mouth.

Hours had passed like minutes. When the lights in the club came up, we were both a little dazed. The furniture was shabby. Some booths sported long strips of duct tape that held the stuffing in where the vinyl had cracked. The velvet sofas and chairs were discolored from many nights' worth of sloshed drinks. I concentrated on the details of the furniture the way some people were noticing their dance partners' smeared makeup or wrinkly shirts—Keon's thermal still looked fresh. We followed the crowd to the bar to close out his tab.

Bar tab settled, we stepped out into the night. I used the elastic tie on my wrist to whip my hair into a bun. "Just add water!" I said, joking about how my hair had gone from straight-pressed locks to free-ranging spirals.

Keon placed his hand at the nape of my neck, where my hair was its curliest. "You look like Chaka Khan . . . It's beautiful."

In my twenties, there was deeper intimacy in the moment a man first saw my natural hair texture than when he first saw me without makeup the morning after. Although I'd grown out the chemical relaxer in my hair years earlier to join the swelling natural-hair movement that encouraged Black women to embrace our kinks, naps, and curls, I still straightened my hair with a flat iron before work. Corporate America hadn't yet incorporated our hair into its business-casual guidelines. I hated that look the old guard gave me when I arrived at meetings in a fluff of curls, my head like a sun-bronzed dandelion gone to seed. That look stayed with me—taut smile, disapproving eyes.

Keon liking my hair meant a lot to me in that moment. So, when he suggested we head back to his place, I said yes. I said yes even though I had a weird awareness of my tampon, the kind that meant it might be full. I was toward the end of my flow, when my period is at its lightest, so I was fairly sure it was just paranoia.

Once inside his studio, it was a quick few steps across the flat brown carpet to his bed. The glass in his window was so thin, I felt like I was standing in the middle of the intersection with cars stopping and going all around me. But Keon's kiss pulled me back into the room. I told myself over and over in my head that my tampon was fine and that it wasn't leaking all over his sheets. That there was not a red rose of period blood blooming across the back of my skirt. When he shimmied down my pencil skirt, I worried about the smell of blood.

He clearly wasn't concerned. He grinded against me; I raced my hands over his chest, dragging up his white thermal as I went. His love of thermals was so unwavering that he'd worn one in warm weather to a nightclub. Dudes who listed "fitness" as an interest on their dating profiles usually annoyed me, but I now found an appreciation for his consistent workouts. Seeing his abs, then his chest, as the fabric rose higher and higher was like lifting the curtain on a PG-13 peep show. Things got R-rated when Keon grew bold enough to slide a hand beneath my panties. I placed my hand over his and shifted from beneath him. "Actually, I should go."

Period sex wasn't a milestone I intended to hit two dates in. It was something I'd never done with anyone. To me, it was the equivalent of having a man over to a messy home. A decade later, I, a grown woman, can now count myself among those who enjoy sex all four weeks of the month. But in my twenties, it was inconceivable. There was too much potential for blood, gore, and odors! The logistics were too involved. It went beyond laying down a towel. *What should I do with my tampon? Do I remove it? Does he remove it? Once removed, is it temporarily placed on the nightstand, or does someone quickly escort it to the trash can like a sanitation-device valet and then hop back in bed? Am I that someone? Is he? Be a good host! If I remove it beforehand, do I make a mad dash back to the bed, trying not to trickle blood on the floor as I go? Do I leave my used tampon behind in his bathroom? What if he doesn't have a trash can in his bathroom?* I wasn't even sure how to gauge a man's interest in period sex—whether I should present it as an option or if I should just mention *I'm on my period* and see whether he would fall back or forge on. I truly used to stress about these things. Now, I just ask. And nine out of ten times, they're down. It turns out, men tend to be less squeamish about the regular goings-on of my body than I'd made them out to be.

And really, that was the issue: my body. Not my period. I had this powerful urge to be in total control when I found myself in vulnerable positions—like half-dressed in a near stranger's bed—and bodies are their own entities that aren't entirely predictable. I've almost completely blocked from my memory the day I learned that imitating plywood during sex is a trauma response. I regularly relied on drinking to loosen me up. Once, while hooking up with a hot British soccer player, I'd felt so awkward, I leaped from bed to grab two beers—both for me. I chugged one, then the other while riding him, thankful my buzz settled in quick enough for me to enjoy myself by the time we flipped positions. As I've identified these sexual hang-ups, I've done the work to put them down, only for more to come a-calling. My aversion to vulnerability continually separates me and my body, me and my emotions. And that night in Keon's bed was no exception.

By the time I'd run a few period-sex scenarios through my head, any sexy feelings I had going on were thoroughly diminished. Respectful Keon didn't even require any specifics about why we had to stop. In minutes, I was back in my skirt, and he was walking me to my car.

♥

Keon's finger-bang technique treated my cooch like a purse he was rummaging around in for bus fare. We were in my bedroom. It was our third date, which meant I was at least making progress toward finding a boyfriend. GRE study guide: still dusty. Credit card bills: still unopened. Forever 21 clothes: still too many popped tags.

I yanked up my dress, sat up a little, and craned my neck, trying to see what was going on down there. Keon took my movements as a sign of interest, and soon, his mouth joined his fingers. He'd shown more enthusiasm eating the chicken I'd cooked for dinner than he was showing the platter between my legs. He was too tame. I wanted more urgency. Keon didn't seem to notice that what he was doing was about as arousing as a gyno visit. He wriggled out of his black Levi's, so I reached over to open the large jewelry box on my headboard. I watched him pull down his boxers, then sifted through the box for an appropriately sized condom.

We were drunk on wine, we were in my bed, and our three dates had gone well, so I decided to see our unsexy encounter through to the end. This was something I generally did because it was somehow easier—quicker, even—to just fuck a dude than halt things, request he change it up and possibly be rebuffed, potentially hurt his feelings, or encounter any awkwardness. Pussy was a renewable resource in a way that my time and tolerance for emotional discomfort were not. At some point, I'd learn that using my words is far easier for me than having mediocre sex, but I wasn't there yet. The few times I had spoken up, men had assured me they knew what they were doing (*Oh, OK, because it really feels like you don't . . .*) or pressed on ahead with whatever was meeting their desires.

I handed Keon the condom. He tore into the wrapper, and I watched as he lost his erection. I pretended not to notice and kissed him some more while he fumbled around in his lap. After a while, he looked at me and said, "Um . . . sorry . . . I don't think this is going to happen . . ."

Outside of the bedroom, we seemed to be heading toward something, and now our momentum was at risk. It was then my turn to fumble as I tried to find the right words. If I couldn't articulate my own body issues, how was I supposed to counsel somebody else through theirs? My search was for the magical man who could help me overcome my life inadequacies without possessing any of his own. Now, I know there are so many alternatives to penetrative sex and other forms of intimacy, but at twenty-seven, I'd been operating on an outdated playbook that'd offered me no guidance. I was entirely unprepared for this scenario.

"It's OK, we had a lot of wine with dinner," was the most I could manage, my hand on his shoulder, eye contact averted.

For our fourth date, Keon had me over. He'd cooked his family's secret gumbo recipe. I think the secret was not adding any seasoning. I could barely hide my frustration when I asked for a bit more rice and he refilled my bowl to the brim with more gumbo. Still, the gesture was sweet; not many men had made me dinner.

We sat thigh to thigh on his old yellow couch, eating our bland gumbo by the spoonful, holding our bowls in our laps. I gestured toward his bookshelf. "Have you read every James Baldwin book?"

"No, not all, but I own most of them."

He didn't ask me, and I didn't announce that I'd yet to read a single thing by Baldwin. I moved Baldwin up on my mental list of writers to read. The last books I'd read were from the Hunger Games series. Maybe I just needed to move reading in general higher up on my list. Why hadn't I read any Baldwin? I was probably too busy exerting my energy on mentally willing fuckboys to text me back.

I finally managed to clean my bowl of gumbo, and Keon suggested we watch a movie. When I saw him perch his laptop on his legs, I asked if maybe we'd be more comfortable on the bed.

Keon adjusted his glasses. "I didn't get Wi-Fi, and the cord doesn't reach that far."

He'd told me earlier he'd moved in a rush. He'd hated his old roommate to the point it was depressing him. This was the only apartment he could find in his price range. I didn't want him to feel self-conscious, so I said, "It's OK. It's OK—the couch is fine."

After the movie, we were free to make our way over to Keon's bed. I was confident we weren't going to have a sequel to the "whiskey dick" episode from our last date; neither of us was drunk. We took turns stripping layers of clothing from each other. I carefully removed his glasses and set them on the windowsill.

Keon swept his hand across the floor, searching for and finding his signature black Levi's. He plucked a condom from his back pocket. Before he could roll down the rubber, again, he lost his erection. He acted fast and dove mouth-first between my legs. I tried to focus, to stay in the moment, but I couldn't stop thinking about why it was happening again. I'd never experienced it with other partners, but all those *Cosmo* mags I'd read back in middle school, before I'd ever even seen a dick face to face, had made it clear: it didn't have anything to do with my sex appeal.

My motions became robotic and stiff. I wasn't sure where to put my hands or my mouth or anything. I was following his lead and avoiding addressing the issue. Out of desperation, he settled for what he had and tried to cram his semifirm dick inside me, which was like trying to put the cookie dough back in the tube. One attempt at a pump, and his dick slithered out.

I was basically an inanimate object at that point. I wished I could just sink into his mattress, through the floor, and down into the apartment below us and run out his neighbor's front door to my car and never look back.

Keon flipped me over. I reared up on my knees, and he approached me from behind. I was grateful I didn't have to look him in the face. Instead, I was staring directly at the family portrait hanging above his bookshelf. He, his mom, his dad, and his siblings were all the same honeyed-cream color as the condensed milk my mom used to pour into my oatmeal when I was a kid. He was now semifirm again, hard enough to penetrate me. Sort of.

Minutes later, Keon's grip on my hips tightened. "Ugnnnnhh!"

I stayed there on my hands and knees for a minute longer, staring at his Baldwin books while I tried to fix my face into anything other than a look of disappointment.

There wasn't enough time to fake an orgasm, but I did my best to fake that warm, glowy expression. When I turned back around, the look on his face was genuine. That wasn't something I wanted to take from him by initiating an awkward conversation. I tried to reach slowly for my dress, but my actions must have seemed hasty because he asked, "Are you leaving already?"

"Yeah, remember, I have that flight tomorrow? I still need to pack and get a little work done."

I turned from him, my expression still shaky. I wasn't lying about my flight, but I was lying about why I was leaving. I walked over to his bookshelf and pulled out a slim, small novel: *The Great Gatsby*. "Mind if I borrow this? I've been meaning to reread it before the movie comes out."

"Sure, of course!" he said, joining me at the bookshelf.

He wrapped his arms around my waist and kissed my cheek.

Finally, I could look at him with a real smile on my face. "Thanks, I'll bring it back to you."

Another lie.

The next morning at LAX, I opened Keon's copy of *The Great Gatsby*. In the margins were notes written in tiny, rigid handwriting. I was delighted to hear his voice in my head as I read his insights: "Gatsby's age . . . Distance from the Greatest Generation?"; "delusions of grandeur"; "Gatsby is reclaiming the past." This felt as intimate as curling up in bed and reading Keon's diary. Around me, LAX was bustling with people boarding departing flights and deplaning arriving flights. At that hour, it was all business travelers wearing creased slacks with their laptop cases slung over their shoulders, leading their roller bags through the airport like little dogs on leashes. Midway through the book, when Gatsby reunites with Daisy, Keon had marked a few lines:

There must have been moments even that afternoon when
Daisy tumbled short of his dreams—not through her own

*fault, but because of the colossal vitality of his illusion. It
had gone beyond her, beyond everything. He had thrown
himself into it with a creative passion, adding to it all the
time, decking it out with every bright feather that drifted
his way. No amount of fire or freshness can challenge
what a man will store up in his ghostly heart.*

I laid *The Great Gatsby* across my lap and dreamed of a world where a man loved me like Gatsby loved Daisy.

I was completely unaware that I was Gatsby. I wasn't writing. I wasn't reading. I wasn't scheming on ways to make my life better. No, the grand illusion of a life-realigning love was my sole creative endeavor. Once I'd read Keon's Plenty of Fish profile, he'd become an essential part of my Black coupledom fantasy, where we attended rallies against police brutality hand in hand, supported Black-owned businesses, surprised each other with concert tickets when bands like the Roots came to town, and argued over whose granny made the best collard greens. Like a "This Black American Life"–themed snow globe with us as the two tiny figurines in the middle, looking up in wonder at the magic floating down around us.

There was no room in my snow globe for who Keon really was. The entire premise of these dating sites was that an algorithm could be used to find a perfect match. That data points could lead you to your destiny. That height, education, and TV choices were enough to filter out the undesirables. At least when I met someone out and about, the delusion wasn't so potent. Men who didn't line up with my ideal partner weren't immediately dismissed like I did with their online counterparts. If we'd already sparked an attraction, everything else had the potential to become inconsequential. And jubilant, reliable sex managed to keep these men around much longer than the shitty ways they treated me warranted.

But I hadn't met Keon at an after-hours spot or in aisle eleven at the grocery store; I'd met him on the internet. So, there he was, my Daisy, with droopy petals.

I reached over the stack of unopened credit card bills on my bedside table to plug my dying phone into the charger and continued talking to my middle sister. "I was at Target picking out a card for Daddy when the guy I'm seeing called me. I started talking about Daddy's gift, and he told me he doesn't believe in gift giving! He says he doesn't give them or expect them. Plus, he says he's a *Marxist*. I love Obama way too much to get serious with a Marxist." Not that I even knew what being a Marxist entailed.

"So, what's the problem?" my sister asked. Her tone was flat, checked out. She was probably at work, staring into an Excel sheet, absent-mindedly keying in shortcuts and equations.

"Well . . . I just realized that we've been on four dates, and he always wears the same outfit."

Her voice rose when she responded. "*What?* I thought you were going to say something else petty and pointless, but that's just weird. I have you on speaker, and my cube mate's jaw dropped to the floor when you said that! Do you think he only has one outfit?"

"No—"

Before I could gripe at her about putting me on speaker without telling me, she cut me off. "So, he just has multiples of the same outfit? That's even weirder! Did you check out his closet when he made you dinner?"

"No, I didn't snoop through the man's closet!"

"I would have," she said. I could feel her cube mate nodding along vigorously. I didn't even tell her the repeat outfits weren't our main issue.

That night, Keon texted that he was outside my building. It was our fifth date. I peeped down at him over the railing. Predictably, he was standing on my stoop in a white thermal, black Levi's, and classic Chucks.

Spring was sprouting into summer, and we walked several blocks to a Thai restaurant. Over pad thai and spring rolls, I asked him if Jack Johnson was the Muhammad Ali of his time. He explained the parallels and differences between the two and the degree to which the society they lived in accepted or rejected each boxer. I was smitten by his mini-lecture.

After dinner, we were once again in my bed, and Keon once again lost his erection. He moved from on top of me and sat beside me.

This was it. Time for some real talk. Or so I'd thought. Instead, he said, "Maybe you could just give me head?"

I wish I could have just left, but we were at *my* apartment. Keon had gotten quite cozy with our situation. Even though I'd played my part in making him comfortable by not addressing the issue at hand, I still couldn't understand how he could continue to initiate sex without saying anything about what was going on.

I didn't push him for an explanation because I wasn't sure how. We were on date five; we were entering possible relationship territory. I was tired of being single; I was ready to go steady. I wanted more meals with dinner conversations about historical Black figures and someone I could discuss books with and who thought I was pretty even when I was a sweaty, frizzy mess. But I also wanted a satisfying sex life. Just not enough to say something. I guess Keon wasn't the only one who figured a relationship where difficult conversations never took place was feasible.

I was at the Room, a super-small, super-dark bar in Hollywood, with a friend, listening to one of our favorite DJs work his way through a Prince set in honor of the Purple One's birthday.

"What do you think it is?" she asked me before sipping her cocktail.

"I dunno—he said he's been depressed a bit since moving out here. Maybe he's taking something for it, and this is a side effect?" It was hard to make out the faces of anyone else in the bar. I scrunched my eyes up, trying to see if Keon's replacement was in the club that night.

"Do you really want to date someone on depression meds?" she asked.

"I mean, I guess I don't care as long as he keeps taking them." I shrugged.

At the time, I thought I was being progressive, nonjudgmental. But really, I was being selfish. I wouldn't mind if he was taking medication because, to me, it meant he'd stay "normal." Never mind that that's not really how depression or medication or even people work. Or that a love contingent on someone never inconveniencing you with their mental health is a stingy, thin love.

"It doesn't matter what the problem is," she said. "You have to stop seeing him." She finished off her drink and set it on the ledge behind the booth. "That whole one-outfit thing is too weird."

It was weird. Really weird. But Keon and I were supposed to go on our sixth date the next day. Shit was getting serious. I wasn't ready to give up on my snow-globe-relationship goals.

"But he's an attractive, educated, young Black man, and he's into *me*."

I was still under the impression that the issue with us was Keon's erectile dysfunction and not our combined inability to be vulnerable. Most people my age have divorced parents who hadn't been great at communicating with each other—or even with us as children. I give them a pass. It was the '90s—a time before gentle parenting. But how many times had I been told "Fix your face" when I was getting emotional about something? Or warned not to ask so many questions? I went from a child who struggled to hide her emotions to a grown woman who couldn't talk about her feelings or ask someone about theirs. And it didn't seem like Keon was any more capable than I was.

The plot of nearly every romance movie hinges on this failure to communicate openly and honestly. Could you imagine in *Love Jones* if Darius had just said "Don't" instead of letting Nina move to NYC? Or if she'd just been honest with him about wanting him to want her? And lack of important talks sells books—why else were so many people eager to let Steve Harvey, a man on his third marriage, convince us there wasn't anything problematic about scheming our way into men's hearts by mimicking their fuckery?

Drake's "Marvin's Room" had dropped the year before. Drake tipsy, pleading with a girl to speak to him. The song was basically my anthem. At various points, I'd been both Drake and the girl on the other end of his drunk dial. You could say the song's about being in your feels after last call, that loneliness, a desire to use intimacy as escapism. But there's also the tension of not knowing what you want, or it being too late to even get what you want, and just general life stagnation. Aside from my progressing series of dates with Keon, nothing in my life felt like it had any cumulative value.

Millennials were the "friends with benefits" generation. Fucking the same guy over and over without it leading to a relationship wasn't that different from paying rent month after month on an apartment you'd never own. Or landing a job in the emerging gig economy, piecemeal work never adding up to a career. No wonder we went out every weekend—the nightclub, our collective pity party. The joy and excitement of being lit as brief as the light flaring off the sparklers on the champagne bottles paraded into VIP by hot chicks.

When I saw Keon over the weekend for our sixth date, he was wearing a black T-shirt and blue jeans. "Whoa, I was starting to think you only had one outfit!" I exclaimed as I settled into his car. We were on our way to an outdoor movie.

"What's that supposed to mean?"

"Well, on our last five dates, you wore the exact same shirt, the exact same jeans, and the exact same shoes."

Keon looked both ways at the intersection and then looked at me before pulling out onto Silver Lake Boulevard.

When he spoke, I thought he might attribute the single-outfit thing to being broke or to being an overwhelmed grad student who didn't have the brain space to think about his sartorial choices—he'd once told me he was often so deep in thought he'd forget to shut his fridge door. Or maybe he'd liken himself to Steve Jobs and the genius's signature turtleneck—a self-imposed uniform as a sign of higher intellect; he was above needing a wardrobe to define him. Or maybe he'd tell me it was the ensemble he felt most comfortable in, the right combination of textures and fit—he'd say he didn't have all the right words to explain why clothing could be a struggle for him, but it'd still be clear enough for me to understand that I should probably stop being so judgmental.

But instead, he said, "What? Who would even notice something like that? It's weird you would notice that." I dropped the conversation.

The movie was at the Hollywood Forever Cemetery. We cuddled on a plaid picnic blanket a few feet from actual tombstones, waiting for *Nightmare on Elm Street* to begin. While the Freddie on the screen escaped from people's nightmares to torture their waking lives, a Freddie impersonator crept through the audience, scaring unsuspecting movie-goers with long plastic talons. There was no escaping the horror. Even after the credits rolled.

At the end of the night, Keon walked me up the three flights of stairs to my apartment. When I unlocked the door, he began to step in after me, but I turned around and stopped him, placing my hand on his chest before he could pass through the doorway. "Actually, I'm meeting up with a friend super early in the morning. We're doing professional pics for my LinkedIn profile." When I saw confusion in his eyes, I added, "I'm not trying to look tired."

I did have an early photo shoot, but I'd left out the part about not wanting to go to bed frustrated. Keon shifted backward. I stared at him, and he stared at me, matching sets of brown eyes. I knew if I'd just let him come in, there'd likely be more dates, and there was a good chance he'd become my boyfriend, thus placing me on that married-by-thirty track.

But I just couldn't. My ghostly heart wouldn't allow it.

We stood toe to toe, his black-and-white Chucks butting up against my wedges. We were like mismatched bookends with too many volumes of secrets between us.

"OK, good night, then," he said.

That night, I probably should have gone to my bedroom, cleaned the popped clothing tags off my floor, sorted my credit card bills, and sat down at my desk to study for the GRE. But I'm sure what I really did was open my laptop, swap out the pics on my dating profile, and wait for my next match. And I probably backslid enough to text Chevy, too.

A couple of weeks after Keon and I had stopped talking to each other, I was in San Diego. Some friends and I had spent the day drinking at a brewery and then dropped by a Mexican restaurant on our way back up to LA. I wasn't driving, so I filled my glass to the brim with frosty margarita. I read off some irate responses from Black Twitter over Gwyneth Paltrow's tweet, "Niggas in Paris for real," during Jay-Z and Kanye's "Watch the Throne" tour stop in the City of Lights. One of my white friends—well, former friend—huffed, then sighed. "Oh, c'mon. It's not a big deal." It was, I insisted. "What? You're telling me if I used that word, you wouldn't be my friend anymore?" I felt the dare in her tone.

I looked at her Black roommate. He looked back at me, exasperated. It wasn't his responsibility to wrangle this white girl; he was only concerned about collecting her half of the rent every month (and sometimes even that didn't happen).

"Yeah, I am," I said. I refilled my margarita glass.

"I just don't see why you care so much about a *word*."

"Generations of chattel slavery in America. More important question: Why do *you* care so much about being able to say the word?"

Drunk and dramatic, I exited the table. I walked to a corner of the restaurant and gave in to my impulse to call Keon. He'd understand. And he did. Soon, he was as riled up as me—exactly how I'd wanted my friends to be.

And then I asked, "So, um . . . about . . . you know . . . Are you on antidepressants?"

"Yeeaah," he said. And I could picture him: elbow bent, rubbing the back of his head and exhaling.

"Why not just pop some Viagra?" I was drunk, yes, but it was still an asshole question.

"I don't want to do that."

"OK, well, thanks for listening to me," I said, then returned to my friends. The remainder of my margarita had gone watery; the conversation at the table had moved on.

Deposited safely at my doorstep hours later, I followed another impulse and texted Keon to set up a seventh date. The night of, he canceled.

I kept his *Great Gatsby*.

Gatsby had sought to pluck Daisy from her life and place her among his bouquet of achievements. Just like a wildflower gone from field to vase. Just like me wanting to check a box. But a person is not a degree. Not a perfect credit score. Not a six-figure salary. They are to be loved, not achieved.

You can trim the stem of a wildflower, liberate its beauty from the dirt tangled in the twisted knot of its roots. But its bloom will fade before its time; its petals will drift away. It is the twist, the tangle, the dirt, the soil that sustains the wildflower, that keeps it free. I'd wanted the beauty of Keon without the tangled knot of who he was as a person, without the complications of what he was going through. I never once asked if being in LA made him homesick. Or how he was doing as a Black man in a PhD program. Or what it meant for him to find his mental wellness at odds with his sexual desires, especially in a society that frequently fetishizes Black men and reduces their masculinity to their sexual performance. Or even just if what he'd needed more than a date was a friend. I never asked, but even worse, I never even *thought* to ask. I'd waited and waited for him to explain himself, expected him to say something. But had I deserved his openness? The appropriate response to "I'm on antidepressants" isn't to suggest a getaway to Viagra Falls. I had failed to see myself and my own life beyond the limited imagination of the American dream. And so, I had failed to see Keon beyond a figurine in my Black American Life snow-globe fantasy.

On our first date, Keon and I had bonded over our shared love of Morrison, but she wasn't who I had reached for on his shelf, and I hadn't yet read what I consider to be her greatest commentary on the lives of Black women and our relationships. When I finally did, I remember, I stroked the page in recognition of the description of Sula:

> In a way, her strangeness, her naiveté, her craving for the other half of her equation was the consequence of an idle imagination. Had she paints, or clay, or knew the discipline of the dance, or strings, had she anything to engage her tremendous curiosity and her gift for metaphor, she might have exchanged the restlessness and preoccupation with whim for an activity that provided her with all she yearned for. And like an artist with no art form, she became dangerous.

In those pages, Toni told me that as a Black woman, I'm here to create. That in the art, I'd find my greatest love affair, my wholeness, and my answer to my lonesomeness. I didn't need to risk my heart—or anyone else's—to pursue an illusion. At twenty-seven, I'd felt both too old to be stuck in the same place and also like I didn't have what I needed to move forward. I thought I was behind on a timeline. When really, I was still so new and already in motion. Unaware that I was never meant to be linear. That my progress in life wouldn't come in a series of checkboxes. I grow like an ocean, swelling with energy. Understanding comes in waves. Then, recedes and returns. Always bringing me back to myself, always knowing—even if I don't always understand.

PART III:
FREEDOM . . . KINDA

Chapter 14

Keepsakes

When I learned my company was relocating me from LA to Denver, I called Tyler to see if he wanted a slot on my farewell tour. We'd moved together, so it seemed right to notify him that I was leaving California. We'd stayed in touch. A catch-up call every then and again. A couple of years after we broke up, we'd seen each other for ice cream. But still, I wasn't sure if he'd want to see me.

The last time I saw him, it'd been awkward. He'd invited me to see his dance crew in a showcase in Hollywood; he'd had a solo. He'd neglected to mention the ten-dollar parking, the twenty-dollar cover, and the fact that his crew wouldn't hit the stage until midnight. It was a Monday night, and I had work at eight the next morning. It also appeared that he'd neglected to mention to any of his friends the exact nature of our relationship. I saw one girl nudge him and smile as if I were to be his next prospect. Another girl asked me, "So, how do you know each other?"

"We moved to California together," I said flatly.

Had he moved on from me so thoroughly, he never mentioned me in conversation? Ever? We'd gone to high school together. Passed whole summers up late, talking. Listening. Kissing. I still knew the address of the house where his mother lived by heart and still used their landline as my rewards card number at the grocery. We'd shared a savings account and four different homes in three different states. We'd packed the car together for our cross-country road trip. Spent two weeks camping out across the nation. Together, we'd celebrated when he was accepted into a scholarship program at that Orange County dance studio. And here he was in a dance crew, and no one knew who I was.

For so many nights after we were over, I didn't sleep on "his" side of the bed or even in the center; I slept only on my side, my body both oblivious to and obsessively aware of his absence. We'd taught each other that with time, heartache could be survived. I hadn't seriously dated anyone since our breakup or called anyone else my boyfriend. Never learned anyone's shoe size or woken up every morning to the same face. Never gotten to that point with anybody else where I'd felt secure enough to wear my feelings for them plain and unadorned, without a protective layer. Maybe he had meant more to me than I had meant to him.

When I called to tell Tyler about my move, he agreed we should get together before I left. I met him in Anaheim, where he lived at the time. He was no longer running rides at Disney, having secured a spot as a performer in the parades—just like he'd wanted.

I wasn't feeling well, so he suggested pho; he knew a place. At the restaurant, the server sat steaming bowls of soup before us on laminated menu place mats. I reached for a set of chopsticks and began adding bean sprouts and cilantro to my bowl.

"You know how to use chopsticks?" Tyler asked.

I was offended and almost snapped at him, "Of course I know how to use chopsticks!" And then I remembered that I had not learned until a couple of months after we broke up. In Kentucky, I had refused to use chopsticks. I didn't see the point. It made eating rice a slow process, and forks were readily available everywhere. But when I worked in Laguna Beach, I would eat at the sushi restaurant in my building once a week.

Every week, I would ask for a fork, and every week, the sushi chef would frown at me. Finally, shame won out over stubbornness. Not only had I learned how to use chopsticks since Tyler and I had broken up, but I'd spent two weeks in Tokyo. While I'd been with him, I hadn't even had a passport or even pumped my own gas. In our time apart, I'd become someone who caught flights alone to foreign lands. It surprised me that he remembered something about me that I hadn't, some sliver of me I'd left behind.

After pho, he invited me back to his house to meet his new puppy, an Australian sheepdog he'd named Dundee after the Crocodile Dundee movies. He led me to his bedroom, which he shared with another dancer, and there were two queen beds pushed against opposite walls; two kennels, one at the foot of each bed; and two desks, each with a computer. At least six dancers lived in the house. It was the only way they could afford to make dancing a priority over making money. One of the only things I was looking forward to about Denver was that I'd no longer need to live with a roommate.

Tyler opened the kennel, and his puppy came running out. We both kneeled on the floor, and after covering Tyler in licks, Dundee took an instant liking to me, chewing on handfuls of my hair and taking swipes at my cheek with his little pink tongue.

I noticed the *Kill Bill* poster above Tyler's desk. "I like that," I said, nodding my head in the direction of Uma Thurman dressed in the iconic yellow tracksuit.

"You would," he said. "It's yours. From your dorm room in college."

"What? Why do you have it?"

"I dunno. I found it in a closet in my mom's house. I always thought it was badass, so I brought it back with me."

"What else of mine do you have around here?"

Tyler shrugged. "I still have the nunchucks you gave me." He got up and pulled them off a low bookshelf by his bed and slung them around a bit. That was Tyler. Yo-yo champion. Master knife thrower.

Best backyard boxer in his neighborhood. I'd bought him the nun-chucks because I knew he'd be a natural at them.

While we'd dated, Tyler and I fought plenty over his terrible memory. And here he was, again, remembering things I'd forgotten. Our breakup had not been an easy one, and yet he'd decorated his room with my mementos. Even after we were no longer together, I was still reading him wrong. Just because he hadn't poured his heart out about me to every new friend he'd made for years didn't mean I hadn't meant as much to him as he'd meant to me. We just had different ways of expressing each other's importance.

We'd been apart long enough by that point to know that breaking up had been right for us. There was no more romance between us, but still—to me, at least—*friend* didn't feel like the right word to describe someone I'd spent my entire early-adult life dating. We'd done a lot of growing up together. And describing us by what we no longer were—as exes—didn't feel right, either. I didn't have the word for us.

When I was ready to go, Tyler walked me to my car. "Wow, this is probably the last time we're ever going to see each other," I said.

He pulled me into a hug. "I know. Weird."

But it wasn't.

♥

The next time I saw Tyler, it was July 2020. I was thirty-five. He messaged me on Facebook. His mom was selling her house; he was in town cleaning out his old room. "There's way too many photos of us." I'd moved home to Kentucky four years earlier.

In my twenties, after my middle sister sold the furniture in the storage unit Tyler and I had shared so I could afford to move following our breakup, everything that was left was brought to my father's house. My life with Tyler had been reduced to a series of boxes. Things that once served as props in our memories—sheets, can opener, vase—had become meaningless. They were now just things. What to keep, what to let go. I'd hated that I'd had to dismantle a life we'd built together by myself.

As I sorted, I came across an old photo of us. I'd taken it in my dorm room in college on one of those yellow Kodak disposable cameras that had a dial to keep track of how many shots were left. We were so close to the camera, none of the room is visible, and it looks like our young faces are emerging from the shadows. He is pressing his lips to my cheek, eyes closed, and I'm looking directly into the camera, a small smirk on my face. I was so startled by the happiness on display in the photo, I slid it under the lid of my Crock-Pot box just to get it out of my sight. Years later, when I was living alone in Denver and finally got around to using the Crock-Pot for the first time, when I lifted the lid on the box, the photo and the happiness startled me all over again.

I decided to donate most of the boxes or leave them at my father's house. I shipped one clear plastic tub to my new apartment in Orange County. Keepsakes I couldn't part with: love notes, greeting cards from over the years, and a binder I'd made in high school dedicated to our relationship. I'd collaged photos and magazine clippings and bright-colored construction paper together to mark special occasions. Our first anniversary. Valentine's Day. Prom. Prom again. Vacations.

Because I was not yet an expert at shipping my belongings from state to state, I didn't know that plastic tubs are not durable. They crack and splinter from being tossed around on trucks and in warehouses. By the time the tub arrived in Orange County, half its contents had spilled out, lost forever. Including the binder, our love story. Life had insisted I begin a new one.

I messaged Tyler back. "Lol I'm sorry?!" I joked. I wanted to see the house one last time, and I was practically already in the car before he responded yes, already driving to him in a summer rainstorm.

We sat on opposite ends of his mother's living room. I listened to stories about his life in LA. He was doing stunts on stilts at festivals all over California, across the country, and around the world. He'd been with his girlfriend for a while, no kids; he didn't think he wanted them—and he laughed when I reminded him how much he'd wanted to be a "young dad" when we were together. He still looked the same, except he'd grown his hair out long. He wore it in two plaits that rested on his shoulders. I told him about what it was like to be back in Louisville and to be a writer. I told him I admired that he'd always known who he was. I was—I am—still learning. I was figuring out how to be committed to myself above all else. He told me he was happy for me.

When he walked me to the door—something he'd done hundreds of times as a teenager but had not done in more than a decade—he asked me if I was hugging or not. This was something people asked each other now. While we chatted, we'd put as much space between us as possible. The moist, mossy smell of summer rain had followed me inside. And I could not put out of my mind the dangers of what else might be in the air, had been in the air since the pandemic had begun in March. But I'd risked seeing him anyway.

The side door was in a corner, wedged in between the wall and the edge of a kitchen counter, and across from the door that led to the basement—the stairs we'd snuck down to his bedroom as high school sweethearts, our hormones stronger than reason. I was standing close enough to him to sense the halting energy of his waiting. It wasn't like that, not like back then. He had a girlfriend and had always been faithful to a fault. It was simply his happiness on my behalf, his ongoing goodwill, his need to express it all by holding me, reminding me he'd forever be a safe harbor. But still, I knew how the soft comfort of his white tee would feel with my cheek against his chest. What it would be like for me to feel sixteen and in love with him again.

"No, I'd better not," I said.

"I understand."

Tyler opened the door to let me leave. It was still storming, so he partially stepped outside into the light of the porch lamp to make sure I made it down the wet steps and to my car safely, watching me move through the night on my own. The hot July rain showered over us both. Like a fever breaking and sweat carrying it away, droplets racing down skin, drying, evaporating, returning heat to air—what once was, no longer.

Chapter 15

LA Face, Oakland Booty

Almost twenty years ago, as an undergraduate at the University of Louisville, I enrolled in a course called "Black Women and the Color Complex." The classroom was small and narrow, with a wall of windows down one side and about twenty desks shoved in tight rows. The room filled up fast. By the time I arrived on the first day, I had to scuttle sideways down an aisle to one of the few empty desks left. I took out my notebook, looked up at the professor, then slowly looked around. It was the first, and only, time in my educational history that every single person in the room was a Black woman.

I listened to my fellow students tell stories about their grandmothers pouring a cap full of bleach into their bathwater, and we studied the history of the brown-paper-bag test that was used to keep elite Black social circles light-skinned. There was a girl who had panicked when our professor mentioned we'd all grow darker with age. "You're not going to be unrecognizable—it's just a few shades," Dr. A had said to calm her. It was the first time I was asked to consider that the attributes I'd been indirectly taught to prize in myself—long hair, light skin, being "mixed"—were not just "preferences" men held; they were beauty standards rooted in whiteness.

Since elementary school, I'd heard different Black boys say that they only liked light skin or mixed girls. To a chubby kid with braces, glasses, and frizzy hair, this felt like at least one thing I had working in my favor. I didn't question it any more than I questioned why blondes were considered hot or why it was better to be skinny than fat—I just accepted it as one more thing that made a woman beautiful or not. When I exited my awkward phase in high school, the conversation shifted from statements about who they liked to questions about who I was attracted to. "Do you date Black boys?" they'd stop me in the halls to ask.

Bussing in Louisville meant that the school you went to wasn't always the school in your neighborhood. You'd ride one bus to a compound, where you'd then switch buses with other students and board the bus headed to your school. I was in classes with kids from all over the city. Other students saw me with my white high school boyfriend, and assumptions were made. They'd only ever seen me with Tyler and none of the Black boys who'd come before or those who would come after.

Learning about colorism in college had done nothing to dispel my belief that I was battling racism by being in an interracial relationship— that would come later. Had Instagram existed during the six and a half years I was with Tyler, I would have absolutely been one of those women celebrating Loving Day—the day interracial marriage became legal in the United States—by posting photos of us as a couple online. When we broke up, I continued to see my dating choices as an extension of my politics. But I found that, like race, the intricacies of desire aren't always so straightforward.

After moving to Southern California, once while I was out in West Hollywood with a group of friends, a bouncer held my ID and asked me a variation of the *Do you date Black boys?* question before handing my license back. There was no longer a white boyfriend by my side—in fact, I was out with all Black women—and yet the question hadn't gone away. The bouncer had read something Other in my features.

For most of my life, men have been treating my face like a carnival game: *Let me guess what you are!* Calling me "exotic"—like a car. Like a rare bird. Like a tropical escape.

His question was one I'd grown to hate. I took it as an affront, as men projecting anti-Blackness on me: *I'm Black. Why wouldn't I date Black men?* But it's possible that the subtext of that question is more complicated than that, that this is a question about value—theirs and mine. Somewhere in their history, not only was the question asker taught to desire lightness and certain features and textures, but some Black men were also taught they were unworthy of such women through their own experiences with colorism, featurism, and classism.

If I rejected the bouncer, maybe in his mind, I would have been validating the narrative that he isn't worthy of women who look like me. But if I'd given him my number, I might have been reinforcing a narrative that privileges me solely based on my features and hurts other Black women by maintaining this harmful status quo. Neither scenario accounts for whether there was any actual attraction between this man and me, or our general compatibility. And we weren't seated in a college classroom where we could tease out the fine threads tangled up in that question—we were out front of a bar with a line of people behind me eager to get inside. So, I told him yes, and then lied, "Sorry, I have a boyfriend."

I am a Black woman. This is a fact, and it is also shorthand. It's not always quick or simple for me to discuss my race and family. Yes, I am Filipino because my mother is Filipino. But like me, my mother's father is Black. She grew up in the Philippines without him. She is fair and takes after her mother, who was Filipino but also Chinese. This means my mother is culturally Filipino. And she didn't experience Black culture until marrying my father and moving to Kentucky to be near his family.

As a child, I didn't even know my mother was Black until I met her father. My dad tracked him down, which was a pretty incredible feat in the '90s—a time before social media, before Ancestry.com—and we road-tripped to where he lived in California. My sisters and I slept in the back of the minivan and ate soggy sandwiches out of a cooler while my dad drove the family straight across the country, only stopping for gas and restroom breaks. My grandfather was so overcome with emotion when he saw my mother, they ushered us children out of the house. I only remember being in his presence briefly, and I never saw him again before he passed.

This is a lot to explain to someone upon first meeting them. And frankly, not everyone I meet is deserving of that much information about me. So, instead, when asked, I say, "My mother is Filipino." I say, "*My mother* is Filipino" because when I say, "I am Filipino," the questions that feel like challenges to my identity come. No, I don't speak Tagalog. No, I've never gone back to the Philippines. I grew up in the South in an all-white neighborhood, and I was the only Black kid in my class until I switched schools in fourth grade. That was enough of a character builder without having to trot kids over to the globe and prove the Philippines was a real place.

I've often felt "Black (and Filipino)." Like Black is my primary identity and my Filipino-ness is ancillary to that. Like because I didn't grow up immersed in Filipino or even typical Filipino American culture, I can only claim being Filipino on a technicality. But just because my experience of being Filipino is niche doesn't make it any less valid. Growing up, my parents were friends with several families made up of military husbands—some Black, some white—with Filipino wives. My sisters and I had a whole pack of kids just like us to run with. We knew not to wear shoes in the house, to etch a cross in the rice before serving it, and that it was time to scatter whenever our moms got angry enough to shout at us in their language. Outside of that bubble, though, I rarely came across anyone with a similar background to my own—the Bluegrass Blackapina contingency is a small one.

In college, I learned that as a light-skinned, mixed-race Black woman, I benefit from colorism, but in Filipino spaces, I'd experienced the other end of the colorism spectrum. Sometimes I wasn't acknowledged at all until it was clear I belonged to my mother. It was actually the support of other Filipino writers who readily accepted me as their own that deepened my grounding in Filipino culture.

I'm often surprised to hear Filipinos I perceive as light-skinned refer to themselves as being dark. To further complicate how I'm seen by others and how I see myself, periodic discourse flares up on Twitter about whether or not the rapper Saweetie is Black. Saweetie, like me, has a Black father and a Filipino mother. Less than ten years ago, the back-and-forth on that same social media platform was about whether or not it was anti-Black for someone to refer to themselves as biracial, a category that some view as separate and removed from being Black. I've been the subject of pages of posts by Black women on a discussion board about whether or not I'm allowed to be a voice on the experience of Black women as someone whose mother is Asian. While I have no interest in excusing the vitriol of those posts, I do understand that in a culture where Black women are underrepresented and underappreciated, light-skinned and multiracial Black women are overrepresented in the spotlight.

I may not have grown up seeing many women who looked like me on the cover of magazines, but I could count on them to be fetishized by the hot rappers of the era.

"Long-haired, thick redbone."

"LA face, Oakland booty."

"With an ass like Serena and a face like Aaliyah."

"Lookin' half-Black and Filipino."

My entire aesthetic is a rap cliché. Seeing representations of yourself constantly sexualized isn't healthy, but it was one of the few confirmations of desirability I could turn to when it was mostly thin white women who were being positioned as worthy of attraction. Even if it's shallow, the shallow end of the pool can still be fun to splash around in when you're not allowed in the deep end.

But after Dr. A's colorism course, I couldn't continue to grasp at rap lyrics to lift my ego without being consciously complicit in the messaging that tells Black women with darker skin they are less desirable. It's more comfortable for me to train my attention on white women's privilege and speak in broad terms when discussing the lived experiences of Black women in America, as if they are all the same as my own, as if we are a single collective. But it's not more honest.

It's taken me some time to piece together what it means to me to be Black and Filipino and how that meaning shifts based on where I'm at and who I'm with. And I've had to make peace with other people having their own assessments based on my appearance and their own thoughts about race and ethnicity. I've had no other choice. I can't keep the questions from coming.

Recently, an editor emailed me to say that the poet Chet'la Sebree had cited me in her new project and would like to send me a copy. I was curious. What did this mean? Which essay had she used?

"You'll see," the editor emailed back.

The slim book arrived by mail a few days later. The cover smooth and raw, like a wall after that first coat of primer. Muted colors. Blacks. Grays. Almost shades of white. An arm extended, a hand poised to grasp something, fingers arched back, hesitant, hovering over its own shadow. The poet's signature in electric violet beneath the title of the book, *Field Study*.

I read it as a meditation, a catalog of ambivalence, about white men she's dated and loved. As I read, I wondered if all Black women—all women of color—see their lovers as commentary on their identities and their commitments to their communities or if most simply see them as the randomness of the universe at play. And there on page 29, my own words,

I learned that awareness mattered a lot more to me than race.

MINDA HONEY

Chet'la has uncanny timing. She had returned my words to me the spring I decided to stop recycling men. It was 2021, and I wanted fresh love interests to fawn over. I'd redownloaded the dating swipe apps, and I was considering no longer limiting myself to Black men. I was thirty-six. Still single. In a small city. I needed more choices.

But I wasn't sure I still believed what I'd written. I now had to ask: When it comes to dating and attraction, what does awareness actually change? But now I was questioning my own awareness rather than the awareness of my partners.

I can personally not exalt in the *-isms*, and I can reject men who are vocal about their "preferences," but what happens when they know enough not to voice them or are driven by messaging buried so deep in their subconscious, they don't even know it's there? I don't know. But I've turned these thoughts over a lot—even questioning whether or not my concerns are just virtue signaling. What am I doing with all this fretting that's actually making a tangible difference in the lives of other Black women? Maybe, in the end, the men I choose to date will always be more about me than anyone else.

When I was still entertaining the possibility of motherhood, I feared the complex such a partner might seed in a daughter whose appearance favored his more than mine. But once I removed children from the

equation, my why for not dating these men didn't just disappear. I have dated men who've revealed themselves to be homophobic and transphobic, and their misogyny soon followed. So, how is that different for a partner that places outsized value on something like the shade of my skin? His colorism is sure to come bundled with even more values that don't align with mine, and I doubt I could trust such a man to continue to love me as I age, if and when my health begins to deteriorate, and through other changes that will come over time.

Looking at Chet'la's book, I was reminded about how certain I'd been that the race of who I dated was less important than how that person loved me. And yet, in the intervening years, I'd decided I was done dating white men. Dating in Denver is probably what changed me.

While in Denver, on a date with a white man I'd met at a hip-hop bar, the man smiled at me charmingly before saying, "You aren't what I expected." He'd asked me out after dancing with me for several weeks in a row.

I leaned in closer. I felt alluring, seated at the bar of that upscale Italian restaurant, sipping a martini. I'd just shared how I'd found myself in Denver, about my career. "Oh? What were you expecting?"

"I thought you were just going to be this freaky-deaky Black chick down to fuck."

Experiences like this and the increased national attention on police and vigilante violence against Black Americans and the general apathy of white America might have made me doubt what divides were possible to bridge in a romantic relationship. When I returned to Southern California for grad school, I wanted to revel in having more variety than the white guys who overwhelmingly represented the available men in the city some call "Menver."

But I should have known eliminating the race factor up front would still leave me with plenty of other complications while dating. Although Denver's Black population is small, I'd also dated Black men while I lived there.

At the same bar I'd met Mr. Freaky-Deaky, I'd danced with a scientist doctor from Uganda. His team was doing something too complex for me to understand while wasted, and I loudly exclaimed, "You're going to cure cancer!"

He asked me to dinner.

At dinner, it was his turn to get loud. He found it difficult to believe I was as old as I was and unwed as I was. "What is wrong with this country? Look around—you are easily the most beautiful woman in this room." If they were offended, the dining room full of white people surrounding us did not let on. "This is the country that made Kelly Rowland get plastic surgery."

For emphasis, he repeated, even louder, "*KELLY ROWLAND.*"

After our one and only date, he pestered me to come up to his apartment. I had to refuse several times before he finally got out of my car. But first he tried to kiss me. I turned my head away too slow, and his tongue—dank with nicotine—dragged across my lips.

I continued to be old and unwed.

There will always be a man questioning who I date and why, and I will always be questioning them in return. I can't choose men, choose monogamy, choose heterosexuality without also experiencing fetishization, benefiting from mixed-race and light-skin privilege, and subjecting myself to anti-Blackness. Maybe what I knew then when I wrote those words returned to me by Chet'la is what I now know again: that I might as well date all men because dating any man isn't easy.

If I pan out, I can see how my dating life is determined by more than just my individual choices. Maybe it wasn't that my partner's general awareness of racism mattered more than the race of my partner. Perhaps, it's that my awareness of misogyny—more specifically, misogynoir—and how it undergirds and can undermine my dating experiences is what matters most. It's an awareness that I can use to protect myself from buying into both colorist and racist narratives about who is and isn't worthy of attraction and about who values me and why.

Around the same time that I was refreshing my dating profile and received Chet'la's book in the mail, I was a professor at a small liberal arts college not far from my home in Louisville. And I was back on campus with Dr. A, who'd left UofL to accept a role as dean. One day she came by my office and asked if I might be interested in co-teaching a course with her. I had to tell her no. Sadly, I couldn't fit it into my teaching load. After she left, I wondered if there was anything I could say to young Black women that would mean as much to them as her class had meant to me. I wasn't sure that I could.

But I have tried.

Chapter 16

A Farewell to Fuckboys

Over time, I began behaving more and more like Chevy. I'd let days pass before responding to his texts. I rarely answered his calls. When he complimented me, I'd snark him. He was going through a hard time. He wasn't working; he'd lost his place and his car. And *then* he became interested in dating me. I was in LA; I'd leveled up my life. I wasn't trying to be with Chevy. I used him as a human palate cleanser in between the men I was legitimately dating.

When work had moved me to Denver, I'd kept texting with Chevy and calling him while drunk. I met a man through a friend, and when I'd asked that man how he'd met his wife, he told me they'd been off and on for years. How she'd always been the girl on the side, but one day, he realized she was "the One." I told Chevy about that man, and he said, "See? That's going to be us when we're done with the games and the bullshit."

A few days later, the man who married the woman on the side started sending me late-night texts. I blocked his number.

Anytime I went back to Cali, I'd see Chevy. We didn't sleep together on those visits. We talked about family and work and our dreams. We went places—during the day, fully clothed. I think we may have even held hands while walking down Venice Beach. When I moved back for grad school in 2014, it wasn't long before I called him wasted from a bar. Carless, he took a thirty-minute Uber ride to Riverside at 3:00 a.m. to see me. "Just make sure you're awake when I get there," he made me promise.

Awake, as promised, I opened the door when he knocked. I was thirty and felt twenty-three all over again when I saw him, but I didn't act it; I didn't joyfully fling my arms around him. I led him directly to my bedroom. The next morning, I sent him to the bus stop with a granola bar and some old Apple earbuds—he'd forgotten his, and the trip from Riverside to LA was going to be a long one. That's how committed he'd been to seeing me. Surely, that meant something? But I didn't know how to stop being shitty to Chevy. Under all my fuckgirl bravado were years of hurt feelings from his rejection.

I continued to ignore Chevy's calls and let days go between texts. Summer break had just started when I got an upset 8:00 a.m. message from Chevy: "You didn't call me back."

I checked it, rolled over, and slept a few more hours before responding, "It's too early to be this angry."

"My mom died."

I called him. But even as he was telling me what happened and what was going to happen next, I wondered, *Are we close enough for this?* We'd known each other for six years, yet when I'd found out during the winter that my mother was sick, it hadn't even occurred to me to call Chevy, much less mention it to him. I'd cried into my beer at a bar with a couple of new friends from my grad program. Maybe Chevy and I were close enough. Maybe there are no rules when you lose your mother.

Over the remainder of that year, I began to take Chevy more seriously. He was saying all the right things. Texting me regularly. "We should try a relationship," I said a couple of months into the new year.

After a literary event where I'd read with my classmates in LA, he was moody. When we got back to my place, he was drinking heavier and smoking more weed than he usually did. I should have asked him if he was OK. I should have asked him about his mother. But I didn't. I'd spent so many years perfecting an emotionless veneer, I didn't know how to crack it to ask him hard questions. Again, I thought about how long I'd known him and how little we knew about how to be together. He needed someone, but because he'd set all these bizarre parameters for our relationship, he was standing right there in my room, sleeping right there in my bed, and was completely emotionally isolated from me.

How could it be possible to press your lips against someone else's hundreds of times but not know how to part your mouth and say what needed to be said? How can you see someone's naked body from every single angle but have zero insight into their inner world? How can a man sweat all over you but not let you see him cry? Why was I letting a man drowning in toxic masculinity lay out our rules of engagement?

But how much of it was me not taking control, and how much was just the way it worked between men and women? I hardly had any friends who weren't putting up with similar levels of fuckery from the men in their lives. Men who didn't seem capable of loving us without baring their teeth at us at the same time.

The rest of the night didn't go well. In the morning, Chevy launched into a story about a woman at his work. How she'd followed him home on his lunch break to smoke weed. She was so into him after that. He couldn't believe she'd gotten the wrong idea. I knew he was telling me a parable about us. Subtext: *This is not what you think it is.*

He grew distant. The following weekend, I split a pitcher of sangria with a friend and texted Chevy. I demanded to know what was up. "What's going on?" I asked.

"I don't know. I'll probably hit up this house party tonight," he texted back.

"Not with your weekend. With us." I'd always had a sense of how tight the emotional tether was between us. That week, I'd felt it go slack. In the past, I would have just let him go MIA for a few months, let the feelings die down, then drunk dial him for the usual. But I'd been serious about wanting more from him, just not serious enough to demand it while sober.

He explained he thought we were keeping it casual and saw each other when we saw each other. I sent him a text as long as a CVS receipt. What he'd described was what we'd had until he'd spent years convincing me he wanted to date me. Insisting he wanted more. Blaming me for why we weren't together. He wasn't responding fast enough, so I called him. "I CAN'T FUCKING BELIEVE YOU!" I shouted.

"I'm hanging up, Minda," he said.

"Why?"

"Because you're yelling at me."

"I'M NOT YELLING, CHEVY," I yelled into the phone. I paused. "You're right. You're right. OK. Good night."

For months, I didn't speak to him. I moved back to Kentucky in 2016 without telling him. When I did finally call him again around Thanksgiving, I'd been drinking and wanted him to know I missed him. I didn't tell him I was lonely and uncertain about my dating prospects. He apologized for his behavior; grieving hadn't been easy. I apologized for not being there for him. We began texting and talking on the phone. Again, things began to escalate. He was planning a trip to see family in August and decided to squeeze in a detour to Louisville.

One night, I was out with friends and a guy I liked. We shut the bar down. The guy I liked wanted me to go home with him. I texted Chevy. No response. I called him. No response. I sent him an angry text about how he didn't respond to my texts. No response.

I went home with the guy. The next morning, Chevy texted that he'd been in a basement bar with poor reception, that his phone battery had died.

A couple of weeks before he was supposed to visit me, he started pressing me about my dating life. Looking back, it's obvious he'd wanted to pick a fight. "Don't you want to be real with each other?" he asked during one of our calls.

"No," I said. "Has this ever been about being real?" With Chevy, it always felt like the beginning of the end. Nothing was real. It was a relationship contingent on ifs. *If* he stopped being a fuckboy. *If* I stopped binge drinking. *If* I could trust him. *If* he could love me.

I admitted I was sleeping with someone. He didn't want me to sleep with the guy again so close to his visit. "You're going to sleep with him and then with me a few days later?" he asked.

It wouldn't have been the first time.

"Don't you want to know about *my* dating life?" he asked me.

"No. It's never mattered to either of us who you were dating," I said.

"So, you don't want to know?"

"Fine. Tell me."

Turns out, Chevy had started seeing his ex again. He'd been with her that night I hadn't been able to get a hold of him. He'd lied to me. And he was lying to her, too. He hadn't told her that he'd be coming to see me. He was essentially angry at me for treating him how he was treating her.

I pointed out that I was free to do what I wanted; I wasn't his girlfriend. "And you never will be if you keep behaving this way," he snapped. Before I hung up the phone, he told me not to act like I didn't care but not to be too mad at him, either.

When that call ended, my feelings for Chevy ended, too. Like a hair tangle giving way, like dried food on a dish coming unstuck, my heart had suddenly, finally, and completely released him. I'd been living like a moth when really, I was the flame.

I'd re-created myself in Chevy's image, and he'd despised me for it. I'd despised me for it. What endgame had I been after? Like somehow, by matching his shitty behavior and apathy, I was going to convince this dude who didn't want to be with me that he did? And then what? We raise some shitty kids together? Or more likely, we move to some deserted island where we spend the rest of our lives debating our top-five rappers and never talking about our mothers. That is not a life.

Your fuckboy doesn't suddenly get it together for you. Instead, you get yourself together and move on up out of relationship purgatory.

I'd been trapped there because I was using fuckboys like fire escapes to race away from my feelings before they engulfed me. I was there, like so many women, with all the fuckboys, the creeps, the ain't-nice guys, the boys from around the corner. The ones with the problems. And I didn't even know it because disrespect in dating is so commonplace. I could write lists and lists, tell so many stories of the men I've let sneak into my life at the seams of old wounds. An anthology of assholes.

And those are the ones I dated. That doesn't include the ones who have been hollering things at me from the windows of passing cars since I was twelve. The men who began grabbing at me in nightclubs after I turned eighteen. The one who looked at me with direct, unmitigated wanting under the white light of a department store just this week. Each one pulling a trigger for trauma without warning. They're all my problem. How am I supposed to be anything but fucked-up over this?

But Steubenville happens. And Bill Cosby happens. And #metoo happens. And #timesup happens. And we all argue over whether what allegedly happened between Aziz Ansari and that girl counts. Because to so many of us, it looks like they were making moves across the same game board we were. And it's made us want to flip it over, pick up the pieces, and start again. And I'm starting to feel a little less fucked-up. A little less like I have to have answers for these problems.

This moment is emotional maturity meets cultural upheaval. I'm learning to own my body and my feelings just as our society's figuring out how to make that a safe thing to do. We're collectively tunneling through the trauma to something new on the other side. And we aren't frightened about what we're going to find because it will be so fucking beautiful.

One Friday in a recent November, I drank too much. Started too early, kept going too late. At a networking event after cashing in a fistful of drink tickets, I sent a text to the guy I was dating. I wasn't sure that I was all that interested in continuing to date him, but it was winter, and it was something to do. He was the guy Chevy hadn't wanted me to sleep with again.

A few days earlier, when I'd tried to have an important talk about the status of us, that guy's hands had wriggled beneath my skirt, his fingers plucking at my tights. He wasn't listening to me. He was talking over me without saying a word. I foisted his hands off me and left after I thought I'd said enough to end what we had, but he'd called me the next day as if nothing had changed.

I'd been upset that he required so much support from me but gave me so little in return. I suppose that's why I wanted him to come to the networking event I'd helped organize. But when he arrived, I made a mild scene. Afterward, I cried at a bar with friends, saying, "I have feelings, too!" I was tired of men I could only date if I kept my emotions in a vault. Later that night, I emerged from the restroom and drunkenly proclaimed I was so emotional because my period had just started.

In the morning, I was appalled by the Facebook posts I had made the night before. The ugliness. Emotional, ranting, half gibberish. I deleted them. I announced I was taking a six-week hiatus from drinking. I broke up with the guy properly. But what I didn't do is what I usually did when my heart took a blow. I didn't call Chevy. The queen of drunk dialing had abdicated her throne.

But I still slip on the crown from time to time. I still binge drink. I still get with the wrong men. Now that I'm older, it's more like a catch-and-release program. It's weeks instead of years. It's their problem, not mine. I'm not fixed, but I'm not broken anymore, either.

Chapter 17

White People's Atlanta

The same year I turned twenty-seven, the job I'd moved up to LA for relocated me to Denver. I'd had less than six weeks' notice to end one life and begin another. I arrived in Denver on November 1.

Denver wasn't LA, and it wasn't Louisville, either. On a map, Denver sits almost dead center between the two cities, between the two halves of my heart. I missed my friends I grew up with and my family in Louisville. I missed the southern hospitality and the celebratory nature of the city during Derby. I missed my hometown nestled right up against the Ohio River, the river that created the steady, easy pulse we all lived by.

I missed LA's endless summer. I missed the new friends I'd made up and down the West Coast. I missed standing on the top floor of a skyscraper and looking out over the city, knowing just beyond the smog was an ocean with waves that chased each other to shore like children playing tag.

In Denver there was land on all sides. *"Purple mountain majesties."* Tall, large, imposing in their beauty. I lived at the base of the Rockies, where North Face and yoga pants were acceptable attire for every occasion. My friend called Denver "White People's Atlanta."

For work, I covered half the state—from Denver west to the Utah border—selling mop buckets and cleaning carts and vacuums and trash cans. Doing demos in the basements of hotels, the hidden hallways in malls. Slipping in through the loading docks of hospitals, waltzing around unquestioned, a stack of catalogs cradled in the crook of my arm. Everywhere you go, someone has sold that something—from the "WET FLOOR" signs to the doorstops to the cleaning spray bottles.

The new position was a promotion, and although there'd been no part of me that was ready to move, for the first time since Cincinnati, I was no longer living check to check. I had a career I was progressing in. My name on a business card. A work phone. A company car. And a credit card I used liberally for client lunches.

My new life was slow to fill with friends, so I shopped for things to fill my apartment. My bank statements were checkered with purchases from Ikea, Bed Bath & Beyond (the final décor frontier), HomeGoods, the Container Store, Macy's, and Target. After work, it made me feel less alone to wander the aisles of brightly lit stores with the growing crowd of holiday shoppers streaming down either side of me. I spent all the money work had paid me for my relocation, which meant I had to stay for at least eighteen months or repay thousands of dollars.

There was an emptiness to all of my newly acquired possessions. I had a couch that seated four that I never sat on. Four chairs and a dining room table and place settings for six, but I ate my meals in bed, my laptop set at a crooked angle, plate balanced on my lap; Netflix my only dining companion. My entire apartment was like the pristine living room my mom kept in the house I grew up in. The furniture was not for sitting, and we were expected to walk cautiously whenever circumstances dictated that we cut across the living room to get from one side of the house to the other. If you so much as bumped an end table, if even one tassel on the area rug was knocked askew by passing feet, my mom could tell. Every evening when I came home from work, my apartment was exactly as I had left it that morning. It was my first time living without a roommate or a partner. Everything in its place, always. Week after week, month after month.

I tried to pass my time in Denver as I usually did—with the wrong men.

It was February 2013, more than a week after Valentine's Day. I met Nick online. A few messages in, we discovered we lived in the same massive downtown-Denver apartment complex, so close to the Rockies' stadium I could hear the roar of the crowd with each crack of the bat. Nick invited me to meet him at the liquor store on the corner. I said yes. I said yes even though I wondered, *Who the fuck wants to meet at a liquor store on a first date?* Decidedly not a meet-cute. But at least it was a reason to leave my apartment.

By the time Nick walked into the liquor store, I was already at the register with a bottle of red wine in hand. He was late. He nodded at me as if we already knew each other. The cashier, who usually commented on how pretty I looked in my driver's license photo, saw the nod and looked betrayed. Nick was barely taller than me, and when I saw him, I remember I didn't immediately find him attractive—something about the shape of his head—but I made the split-second decision to like him anyway.

Outside of the liquor store, his dog was tied to a rail with an old belt looped around its neck. He'd had his dog for quite some time, but for some reason, he didn't own a leash. I didn't say anything.

"My apartment's messy, but you're welcome to come over and kick it," he said as he freed his dog from the railing and wrapped the end of the belt around his fist.

I didn't know this guy, so I wasn't trying to be alone with him in his dirty-ass apartment. My place was clean, but I wasn't ready to have this stranger over. Instead, I suggested we hang out in the communal area of our apartment complex. Complexes that advertise themselves as "resort-style living" always have these oversize living room/rec area types of spaces decorated like a page out of a Pottery Barn catalog, with overstuffed couches, vases with dramatic fake floral arrangements, too-large coffee tables with too-sharp corners, a supersize TV with all of the channels, and some overly complicated beverage machine that serves every variation of coffee you can imagine—if you can figure out the right order to hit the buttons in. There's almost never anyone using this space.

Within the hour, Nick and I were curled up so close on the couch, any closer and we'd have been cuddling. Drinking together can quickly close the distance between you and a stranger. I told him about my move. He told me about where he grew up in Baltimore, his work as a pot farmer, how few Black people there were in the industry. How growing weed had always been a side hustle for him, but after college and after he tired of office work and the East Coast, he decided to move to Colorado to make it a full-time venture. He was good at it.

He drank his beer. I drank my wine. We kept trading little parts of our stories. He was thirty-five. And I'd turned twenty-eight a month earlier. I was five years older than the women he usually dated. And, he felt the need to inform me, they were usually white. He told me about girls from his past, his cheating ways. Telling me, without telling me, not to fall for him even as he pursued me. In the end, I would remind myself I walked into this knowingly.

We kept drinking. My brain bobbed on a vino sea. I refilled my glass. His beer gone, he asked me for a pour, but the bottle was empty. He told me, "I like that you drink." I knew what he meant. Aside from my situationship with Henry, I'd never really dated anyone who didn't drink; I wasn't sure that I could. It would mean always wondering if he was judging me for that second, that third, that fourth glass of wine.

It was past my bedtime; I had work in the morning. Nick rode up in the elevator with me. He got off on the second floor and held the door open while he asked me out. "There's this spot that does hip-hop music—good hip-hop—on Fridays if you want to go." He gave me his number. The doors closed, and I rode the elevator up one more floor.

That Friday, Nick came to my door. When he saw me, his eyes glowed in appreciation. He stepped into my apartment, and his Jordans left two shoe-shaped patches of dog hair on my welcome mat. I hadn't even realized clumps of dog hair could travel like that. "Don't you have a vacuum?" I asked as I motioned toward the floor.

"No," he said.

"You have carpet. You have a dog. But you don't have a vacuum?" His entire apartment must have been covered in overlapping layers of dog hair; he had been living there for more than a year.

"I should get a vacuum," he said. I didn't offer to sell him one.

We went downstairs to wait on a cab. There was a half-inch dusting of snow over everything; tiny flecks glittered in my long hair. I pulled my beanie down low over my ears. The cab never came, so Nick drove us to the bar. He offered to let me out by the entrance, but I told him I didn't mind walking with him. The Meadowlark was in a basement, down a steep set of snow-frosted stairs. Nick bought us beers, and I piled our coats, gloves, and scarves on an empty table. The music was good, and I was happy, beer in hand, boy on arm.

After a while, Nick said he was headed out to the patio to light up. Smoking weed wasn't worth standing out in the cold, so I stayed behind. A few songs passed, and I decided to see what was happening outside. As I ascended the stairs, I could see Nick by the outdoor bar. He was sharing a joint with a few people. I looked at the two girls by his side. I was used to being the girl who made her way over to the guy with the weed at a party, not the girl who was with the guy who brought the weed. Now, I knew why that girl always looked like she was ready to leave. I had just met Nick, and already I felt anxious when his attention wasn't completely focused on me.

I wasn't interested in smoking weed, so I couldn't really join the circle without coming off as clingy. I hovered around the outer edge before finally heading back down to the dance floor alone.

Back at my apartment, I changed the sheets on my bed. Nick didn't help; he stood in a corner of my half-dark room and watched. He looked like a shy teenage boy, uncertain of his next move. I had bought some sheets on sale. When they arrived, they were mostly polyester, and Drunk Minda could not entertain the idea of sleeping on those sheets one more night. When I was done, I looked at him and waited.

"All right, good night, Minda," he said, then headed down to his own bed.

I locked the front door after him and climbed into bed, confused but unconcerned by his decision. Later, he would tell me he didn't stay because he really liked me. Liked me beyond guy-and-girl stuff, liked to be around me. But, he said, he knew we couldn't escape the "specter of the dick." It ruined most of his friendships with women, and he was stalling the inevitable.

Early the next morning, I again opened the door to Nick standing on my welcome mat. A wave of heat rolled over him, and he flinched. "Why is it so hot in your apartment?"

I explained that sometimes when I was drunk, I came home and turned the temp up to eighty. I wanted to feel the heat pressing in around me as I slept. I wanted to be warm. I wanted to feel less lonely—but I didn't say that last part to him.

"What are you doing? Let's get breakfast."

On our way out of the building, we passed the polyester sheets I'd ripped from my bed the night before, stepped on and dirty. Had I flung them into the stairwell? I'd been too drunk the night before to remember.

In Denver, I drove hundreds of miles every week. To and through towns that were or would become shorthand for the tragedies that happened there: Columbine, Aurora, Colorado Springs. I met up with reps in old coal towns that were now blocks and blocks of casinos.

I visited the ski resorts—Breckenridge, Vail, Aspen—in the offseason, the snow on their slopes thin, large patches of grass visible. Once, I rode around with a distributor rep who complained about how her white children had to sit in classrooms that were now mostly populated by kids who only spoke Spanish, the children of the workers who kept the resorts running. I replied that my mother was an immigrant, that I myself had been born elsewhere, that my first language was one I'd long forgotten how to speak. I was not surprised when the topic changed.

Another rep informed me the person in the role before me had taken her to at least one fancy lunch a year, so I obliged. She was older, a woman who'd been in that male-dominated industry for decades. The deep booth, her lips parted to share her wisdom—it all almost felt conspiratorial, until she asked me, "What are you? What are your parents?" Politely, I responded, "My mother is Filipino."

"Is your father Caucasian?" she asked next. She was white herself, and her aversion to the word didn't make the conversation any less offensive. I told her he was Black. She looked confused. "But you have such pretty features!" The server who'd just arrived to refill our waters spun around and walked away quickly. Why couldn't my beauty be owed to my Blackness?

It was a beauty that made men either underestimate my ability to do my job or disregard that I was there to do a job. They'd come by my table at vendor fairs and openly hit on me. One man told me he'd want to spend more time with me, go to the movies, have coffee, if only his wife wouldn't mind. During vacuum demos, I'd show how easy ours were to unclog, and a maintenance man would exclaim, "Look, it's so easy, even a woman can do it!" Building engineers, always men, would sigh and ask if there was anyone else they could call about their faulty faucets. I'd fix their faucets in less than ten minutes and be on my way, knowing better than to wait for an apology. When I showed up anywhere with my male colleague, clients would treat me like his assistant, and he'd feed into it by attempting to task me with things like ordering the lunches—to his dismay, I'd decline.

In the long drives between meetings, I tried to clear my mind. Turned up the radio—that was the year Beyoncé was drunk in love. Trained my eyes on the landscape. The mountains could be seen from almost anywhere, and when I was in the mountains, the scene was sometimes like a frozen tundra, snow deep and dense, trees and bushes and the ground grayed out. The air cold and dead. I imagined getting out of the car and screaming. My voice carrying for miles. And still, no one would hear me.

I wandered through Nick's warehouse while listening to him list the reasons we should never date. I nodded at each one. Each one made sense. His cheating. His lifestyle. His overall fear of intimacy. But when had logic ever stopped me? I'd done this before with other boys, bypassed their every warning. I didn't let my failures dissuade me from repeating my mistakes.

Nick took a picture of me in his forest of marijuana—his babies grown up taller than me. The plants' pointy leaves left traces of their scent on my coat and in my hair. The yellow-tinted lights on the floor, angled upward, gave a lemon-lime haziness to the room.

Nick told me he'd always been drawn to vice. He would sell the occasional dime bag to a friend, but mostly he moved larger quantities—$30,000 to $50,000 of weed at a time. He was a grower, the direct connect, a wholesaler. He'd call me to come down and help him count the money after he'd finish a deal. I could smell the weed before I even reached his door. No one ever complained. It was Denver, the city that would soon legalize marijuana for recreational use.

Just like all the other messy men I'd dated, Nick was drawn to me for the normalcy I provided. He would text me as much as twenty times a day, unable to make a decision without my input. Every mundane thing, from what he should eat for lunch to what he should do with the shorts he ordered in the wrong size to where he should get a haircut. It felt nice to be needed. He wanted to hear my views on current events and what I thought of so-and-so's latest mixtape. He shared my passion for trying out new restaurants and would treat me to meals at the places I recommended. I would match those meals with fancy home-cooked dinners. Crab cakes with homemade lime aioli, slow-cooked Korean ribs, and scallops seared to perfection. He sat across from me at my table—finally, a reason for two place settings—and ate every bite, every time.

One night we did Molly. We rubbed the fine, bitter powder into our gums with our index fingers. Then we went to the aquarium, unaware it was hosting a high school prom that night. Yet for some reason, it was still open to the public. Girls with corsages and boys in dress shoes, playing grown-up. We wandered around the massive curved-glass tanks in awe of the Day-Glo fish, our serotonin receptors crackling.

Back at my apartment, Nick murmured into my pussy, "I just want to make you happy." I wish he'd been staring into my eyes when he'd said it. I took a long hit from his vape pen and let him. Joy began to radiate from below my hips like a triple-X Care Bear stare.

One time in bed, Nick told me he was afraid he was going to die young. Heart disease ran in his family. He wanted me to have his babies, he said, because "you're genetically diverse. Our babies would be pretty and smart." Black and Filipino—he called me a racial hybrid, like I was one of his plant strains. I rolled my eyes.

He told me he'd buy me a flower shop. He'd use it to launder his money. I could run the shop, raise the babies, and write my book. This proposition did not include a marriage proposal. He said these things into the back of my head, the sound of his voice softened by my hair. He got like this sometimes after drinking.

"When you die"—*or desert us,* I thought—"there'd be no money to support your babies or me; you got an all-cash business." I continued without looking back at him, "There's zero incentive for me to marry a man who says he's going to die young."

Nick pulled me closer and said with no malice, "Don't be surprised if you catch a baby in your sleep." Then he was asleep, snoring into my pillow.

Whenever our dating began to drift toward the stability of a relationship, he would go missing, my texts would go unanswered, and he would resurface days later, wondering if I had cooked anything. They say that food is the way to a man's heart, but they don't say how to stay there once the novelty of your cooking loses its allure.

When I was with Nick, I'd smoke weed until I was so high, I couldn't do anything but put myself to bed. It was too hard to move my limbs, like I'd been treading water all day, like I'd been treading water for months. I didn't drink every day—like Nick did—but I drank more days than I liked. I drank until I would wake up in his bed and not know how I got there.

One night we were making out on his couch, and Nick paused to tell me that sometimes this crazy bitch showed up in the middle of the night and pounded on his door looking for him and to just ignore her; she would go away after a while. I should've known then that the night was coming that I'd be that crazy bitch. BOOM. BOOM. BOOM. The side of my fist against the front of his door. No answer. I'd hear his dog inside, whimpering for me.

My California friends would call and text, and they'd all have the same thing to say: "We've never seen you get this way over a guy." I felt trapped in this gray space, trying to tug Nick into my life and steadily slipping further and further into his. On the nights he broke our plans,

I would crank the heat up in my apartment, bury myself under the covers, and wait for Denver's endless winter to be over.

Nick called me and asked if he could come up and sleep in my bed. It turned out, *sleep* was not code for *sex*. He really just wanted to nap at my place. We went to dinner afterward, and the sidewalks were slick with ice. I held on to his arm to keep from sliding around. After dinner, we walked across the street to a pub to get a to-go order for a houseguest he had. I complained that the food was taking forever, and Nick asked, "Why are you in such a rush?"

"I've got to get up early for work, and you have your trip, so we need to get home soon if you'd like to—"

"I just wanted to spend time with you before I left," he said, cutting me off. "Why does it have to be about sex?"

"Is this supposed to be about more than that?"

He didn't answer. He didn't say anything else at all. A server finally came out with the order, one hand under the plastic bag to support the take-out box. Nick tipped and we left.

Later that night, Nick stood in the doorway of my bathroom, outlined in light in the darkness. I raised my head and squinted at him.

"I just had the scariest experience of my life," he said.

Sleep gummed up my thoughts. "But I just cleaned that bathroom."

He said he'd had a heart attack. He'd fainted. He could have fallen face forward, cracked his skull open on the tub, but he'd fallen to the side, into my walk-in closet, onto the carpet. I told him to go back to sleep.

"You're fine," I said. But I was worried. I turned my back to him in bed and stealth googled the signs of a heart attack on my phone. They scared me. He'd left the light on in the bathroom. I got up to turn it off. The faucet was still running, the knobs not quite turned all the way. There was water all over the counter. A ribbon of toilet paper on the floor. I sopped the water up with a bath towel before climbing back into bed. We lay stiffly on our sides, back to back, neither of us sleeping, neither of us moving, until the sun crept up over the mountains.

"I think you need to see a doctor," I said, knowing that he wouldn't, knowing that he had a flight to New York to catch.

He sent me a text from the airport. He was so disoriented, he'd missed his flight; he'd have to catch the next plane out. I badgered him to call a doctor; he said he would when he returned. I worried that would be too late. I thought about the stories I'd heard of shit like this happening to people, how they'd just brush it off and drop dead a few days later.

Finally, weeks after his trip, he called Denver Health. A nurse told him what he'd had was a panic attack. She advised him to stop smoking weed and stop drinking so much. He didn't do either.

My baby sister came to visit. I took her to a concert at Red Rocks. We complained about the burning in our thighs as we scaled hundreds of stairs to reach the open-air amphitheater couched in large poppy-colored slabs that jutted up all around us. From the top, in the distance, the city of Denver, backlit by the setting sun, looked like the dawning of a new civilization. We took hits off a joint passed to us and passed it back. It was the first time my baby sister had ever seen me smoke weed.

When we got back to my apartment, as I turned my key in the lock, my sister told me she preferred weed, that she hardly drank because alcoholism runs in our family. "There's a one-in-three chance, and there's three of us," she said.

It's actually one in four. I thought about telling her, "Don't worry, it's me," to make her feel better, but I didn't because I was afraid it was the truth.

One day, in the car, I heard one of those Snapple "true fact" commercials on the radio. In Denver—5,280 feet above sea level—the sky really is bluer. I silently asked the radio if the blues were bluer, too. I'd never been lonelier. Unable to find work fast enough when my position in LA was eliminated, I'd had no choice but to follow my career to

Denver. And I was quickly becoming the top salesperson in the region. But no matter how many sales I closed or how many months passed, I just couldn't see myself in Denver, even as I was there, attempting to live a life.

Every other professional Black woman I met was equally lonely and counting down the days until they could leave. And they did. One after the other, until I was the only one left from the small social circle I'd formed. I was less than a year from turning twenty-nine. Was this really how I was going to close out my twenties? Single. Friendless. No family nearby. I was somehow even more lost and unsure than I'd been that first year in Orange County.

It was May. Finally, it was warm for real, for days and days in a row. That Sunday, Nick was supposed to pick me up and buy us bikes so we could join this Wednesday-night happy-hour group that pedaled between bars all summer. He texted me midmorning. "Hey, I decided to go drinking. I'll hit you up when I'm home and then we'll go."

Winter was over, and I felt the deep freeze down within me begin to thaw and crack. When I first met Nick, I was lonely. That was my excuse. I was so alone in Denver. But months later, with Nick in my life, I was still lonely, except now I was lonely, and I was sad. It was a second-hand lonely, like Toni Morrison had handed to Hagar over Milkman.

I told Nick I wasn't waiting for him to come home drunk.

But really, I was waiting. I was waiting to see what he would do. I let my anger run different scripts for how this would play out. He didn't text me back.

One of the girls from my bowling team—Did I mention how lonely I was?—texted me to meet her at an arcade bar up the street. I saw Nick before I saw her. He ignored me. He might have thought I'd shown up where he was on purpose. I don't know because he refused to acknowledge me. He was already talking to the girl he was interested in for the night. She looked young.

I got a text from a different bowler: "We're drinking for Tye's b-day over by your place, come over." So, I went. And I drank cocktails that were more vodka than anything else. I'm sure the people at that party, who I hadn't met before, didn't like me because I was drinking all their booze and not even pretending like I wanted to get to know them. I was too preoccupied with sending Nick angry texts.

The next morning, I woke up in bed alone and cringed. As I scrolled through my texts, I could barely stand to read them. One text read, "You're a 35-year-old alcoholic pot farmer!"

I sent Nick an apology. He said he'd told his friends I'd sent him that text, and they'd said they'd be making him a T-shirt because that shit was true. "You want to buy bikes now?" he asked.

"No."

"Why not?" he texted back.

I tried to explain that I was sorry for who I was the night before, that that wasn't me. The past few months hadn't been me. Denver wasn't me. Sober, drunk, in between, I just couldn't keep doing this with him, to him, or to myself. This wasn't a real relationship. He was just someone who wouldn't question my drinking or force me to do something about how unhappy I was. He'd readily forgive me for every fucked-up thing I said or did; all I had to do was accept the same. It was an unconditional love that wasn't any kind of love at all.

I was twenty-eight, and I'd spent too many years dating these hard, prickly men and treating their hearts like crab legs—trying to crack them open to consume what was sweet and tender inside. But I couldn't love these men tender without becoming hard myself. I needed to focus on cracking myself open and finding out what was inside me.

Nick didn't believe me. He texted me every few days to see if I'd forgotten—I didn't forget. I went to the gym. I made friends. I came up with a Denver exit plan. I still drank, but not as much. I bought my first self-help book. I learned terms like *toxic*. Like *dry drunk*. Like *enabler*. Like *golden child*.

Sometimes, he called me drunk in the middle of the night. I mostly didn't answer. But sometimes I did.

"I know for a fact she was older than you because I saw her license when I fuc—" Click.

"I miss you. I'm so sorry. I'm just sitting here waiting for the strippers to show up and—"

Click.

"Why are you being like this?" Click.

He threatened to come upstairs and pound on my door, but he never did. He came up with excuses to see me—he needed to borrow my phone charger; he was locked out—but I didn't come to his aid. Whenever he passed me in the building, it was as if we were strangers all over again. Sober Nick didn't want me back the way middle-of-the-night Drunk Nick did.

Almost every day until my lease ended, I had to cruise past his parking spot on my way to mine. I obsessed over cars I didn't recognize in his space, over his passenger-side visor left down. Another girl?

I knew I needed a change. I used my time left in Denver like a life time-out. In LA, there'd been so many distractions. I could easily avoid having to figure out what I really wanted to do with my life. But in Denver, I had fewer friends, and the cold meant I spent more time holed up in my apartment.

For his eighteenth birthday, I had put Tyler in his first dance lessons. They were taught out of a studio in a rinky-dink strip mall whose parking lot we'd once watched a car chase sling through, but still, the lessons were something. They showed that I believed in his dream. I believed in his dream in a way that I had not believed in my own. Why hadn't I used that money to put myself in a writing workshop at eighteen? I'd been eager to move to California, where he could be around other dancers, but I'd never thought about moving to NYC to be around other writers. What was it about his dream that had felt so compelling, more possible than my own?

I signed up for writing workshops. I spent money on entering a writing contest. My essay came back with a handwritten note about how it wasn't necessary that my work be so raunchy. I kept writing anyway. I opened the GRE book, the same one that'd sat dusty on my desk in LA. I studied for months. I still bombed the math portion. I applied to grad schools anyway. I moved into a cheaper apartment to save money. And then came the acceptance letters.

I needed to tell my manager that I'd be returning to California in a month to attend grad school in the desert, but when I called, he didn't answer. I left a voice mail for him to call me back; it was important, I said. My manager and I had a good relationship, but we rarely spoke. My first year in the role, he'd only called me twice, and once was to ask me whether he should get an iPhone or an Android for his new work phone. The other time was to see how my vacation in Costa Rica had gone.

Once, a distributor rep called me to bawl me out on a Friday afternoon for messing up his order. He hung up angry, told me he was calling my manager next. My panic response was to crawl into my closet and kneel among my shoes, like I was doing one of those earthquake disaster drills we used to do in school. I was certain I'd be fired. When I finally got up the nerve to call my boss, he chuckled and said, "He'll get over it." Turns out, I wasn't even the one who'd messed up the order; the rep had.

This was always my manager's response whenever I made a mistake; he'd shrug and tell me it was a lesson learned. I'd spent my entire work history attempting to prove that I was capable, that I deserved success and opportunities. There was no room for mistakes when someone could decide based simply on who I was—Black, a woman—that I didn't belong. But now I had someone who didn't need convincing, who already believed, who allowed me to fail and learn from those failures. My manager didn't worry about me, and it turns out, he didn't have to—I ended up being the top salesperson in our region within my first year on the job. In addition to a hefty commission check, the company gave me a $500 gift card. So, I bought my own bike. A heavy Dutch-style beauty in a deep evergreen.

The same day I'd tried to tell my manager I was leaving, my coworker invited me to lunch. He was a conservative white man a couple of decades older than me who'd appointed himself as my mentor, even though I was outselling him. He'd once gifted me a dusty copy of Dale Carnegie's *How to Win Friends & Influence People* and lectured me on the importance of appearance and what it said about you in the workplace. Something he thought that I, a twenty-eight-year-old woman, had somehow never considered.

Once, it'd been raining out, so I decided not to bother with flat-ironing my hair and arrived at a meeting in my natural curls. "Your hair . . . ," he'd said, then went silent where the compliment should have been. I could tell from his taut smile and disapproving eyes that he didn't like it. But I didn't care.

I decided to completely stop straightening my hair. The air in Denver was drying out my skin, and my hair was damaged and breaking off. My coworker's disapproving looks kept up until our manager saw my natural hair and told me how much he loved "the look."

My coworker had asked me to lunch because he was upset that our manager had sent out an email congratulating me for a major sale. It was as if he'd thought I'd sent the email out myself, and he chastised me for not thanking those who'd supported me in the work win, like it was an Oscar acceptance speech or something.

"Like who?" I'd asked.

He'd wanted credit.

"For what?" He hadn't helped me close the sale.

He told me that as my "mentor," he wanted to offer me some advice: I needed to be more "humble." *Lean In* was one of the most popular books of the moment, and here he was suggesting I do the opposite. Six years earlier, I'd gone to that lunch with my racist manager and quit my job at her recommendation. I hadn't felt like I had any choice, not really. But that day, seated on a patio with that man, I did have a choice, and I'd already made it. I didn't have to let what he thought define me.

Our manager returned my call in the middle of our conversation, and I excused myself to tell him about the full ride I'd received to attend an MFA program. There was nothing left for me to prove to corporate America. Selling the most trash cans or mop buckets or vacuum cleaners didn't really matter to me. It was time to focus on what I actually cared about.

I quit my job. Gave back the company car. Returned to California and supplemented my small stipend with my bonus check. When I'd seen Tyler before I moved to Denver, I saw how he was living with all those dancers, and I couldn't imagine that life for myself until I was standing at a bus stop in the heat and dealing with roommates who left old food in the fridge so that I could afford to make writing a priority over earning money.

Maybe it's never too late to get over your own bullshit, over your fear, and be honest about what you really want.

On my thirtieth birthday, I rented a car and drove from Riverside to Orange County for dinner at an all-you-can-eat Korean BBQ spot. The lights dimmed. The servers paraded over to the table, and everyone began to sing to me. The table seemed to stretch on forever and ever and ever. And there they were, my friends, loud and joyful. It was like I was turning twenty-four all over again, another new start—but this was thirty. This was something different; I was someone different and ready for whatever was to come next.

Once I received my degree, I was finally ready to move back to Kentucky. It was 2016. That same year, a friend's brother needed a cannabis industry connection. I called Nick. He still had the same number. His voice was bright; there was no hardness there toward me. He'd left Denver, too. He didn't grow anymore. Now, he owned a series of dispensaries. I heard the baby burbling in the background even before he told me he'd become a father. I remembered Nick once showed me a photo of a Black woman from back home; she was his age, fifteen years older than the white women he'd told me he typically dated. She was the one who'd gotten away and the one, I believe, he was quietly praying had been waiting on him to get over his own bullshit, to be ready for whatever was to come next. I pictured the baby on his lap—his cheeks, her nose—and I wondered if she'd been able to do what I'd been unable to do for any of the men who'd wanted to love me but hadn't yet been ready. I wondered if she'd waited for him.

Chapter 18

The Obama Years

On Election Night 2008, I was at a bar in downtown Huntington Beach with a woman I had not been friends with for very long and would not be friends with for much longer. A woman who would have otherwise slipped from the strata of my memory without notice. Now, forever suspended in the amber of my recollection in a *Where were you when . . . ?* moment.

Where were you when a self-described "skinny kid with a funny name" was elected the next president of the United States of America? Where were you when your nation chose as a leader a man with the same skin tone as yours and an equally complicated racial makeup?

This current-going-on-former friend and I were the only Black people in the bar and, seemingly, the only two watching the election results come in. Everyone else was crowded in the back, maybe around pool tables, fists wrapped around beers, clothed in Affliction tees. Someone once told me Huntington Beach was the Klan capital of Orange County. I didn't ask why. I didn't need to. It didn't matter if it was true or not. It was a warning that California was not the beautiful utopia I'd been led to believe it was. That racism's existence hadn't been confined to the South any more than my own existence had.

It was the same night I'd watched Obama, on a TV screen, give the acceptance speech about America being a place where all things are possible. The one in Chicago. With Michelle and the girls. And the snowflakes. I remember calling my granny. A Black president . . . Did she ever think . . . ? How did she feel? "Minda-a-a-a," she said when she answered the phone; she used to always hold out the *a* in my name. Then she compared me to Michelle. "You the only one I know who could pass the background check."

I laughed. My granny didn't know I went out drinking with friends six nights a week. Taco Tuesday. Wine down Wednesday. Thirsty Thursday. Friday was Friday. Saturday was Saturday. And Sunday Funday was spent on the Newport Beach peninsula, drinking from 10:00 a.m. until we blacked out. On Monday, we went to work, and on Monday nights, we rested. I didn't want to be in the White House, a president's wife. I was twenty-three, and the place I wanted to be most was drunk on a dance floor, flirting with a fuckboy. And now, I was free to do so. I'd cast my vote, done my part to put a man in charge of our nation who was going to save us all.

Months later, a Polish friend and I left a nightclub in ritzy Newport Beach. We were headed for my car when an older white man in white slacks lounging near the open door of a white Escalade on rims attempted to beckon to us, leered at us, got rebuffed, and in response, called me a—"Nigger!"

He expected the word to snap in the air over me like violence. Scare me back into my place. But that word off his parched tongue in that beachside city where I had just emerged into the cool night, sweaty from dancing, supremely desired, my body my own dominion—no. He did not get what he wanted.

Instead, I doubled over in laughter as far as my minidress and sky-scraper heels would allow and howled out, "Your president!" with all the bombast of the full five minutes and twenty-nine seconds of Jeezy's presidential anthem crossed with the same energy as the rebuttal to a playground taunt—*Yo mama!* I was young and fine and free and wore my Black president like an invincibility cloak. Feminism had taught me my body was my own, and a Black president made it feel safer for that body to be Black.

I didn't vote for Obama the second time. But I'd wanted to.

It was 2012, and I'd officially moved to Denver on November 1. As far as I knew, this made me eligible to vote in Colorado, where my vote would have mattered more than in deeply blue California. I dutifully showed up at my polling place on Election Day, an indie bookstore, and got in line. When I finally reached the front, the poll worker didn't have my name listed. We went back and forth about whether or not I was eligible to vote; then she sent me over to some government building downtown to plead my case.

The woman there explained to me that I would cast my vote that day, and then it would be sealed in an envelope. Days after the election was over, while they tallied up the ballots coming in from overseas and the votes from people who chose the absentee option, my case would be reviewed. If it was determined I'd had the right to cast my vote, the envelope would be opened, and my vote would be counted. If it was decided that I was ineligible, the envelope would be destroyed. She gave me a slip of paper with information about the website I should check in ten days.

In my short time in Denver, I'd met a woman who was campaigning for Obama, and she'd invited me to an Election Night party at a downtown hotel. The ballroom was massive and mostly empty; I couldn't tell if I'd arrived too early or too late for the festivities. I was in a place in between one thing ending and another thing beginning.

The news had been reporting that an Obama second term wasn't a given. I'd been anxious about it, especially after all the uncertainty around my vote, but Colorado and the nation were both called for Barack Obama. He'd won by a landslide. The ballroom filled with people. Mostly in business casual, mostly people I didn't know. I politely sipped my cocktail, then headed home like a responsible adult with work in the morning.

After the buzz around the election had died down, I visited the website I'd been told to check to see if I'd contributed to Obama's win. The site gave me an error message. Status of my vote? Forever unknown.

In 2013, when the George Zimmerman not-guilty verdict came down in July, I'd been living in Denver for nine months. It was a city where the overall absence of Blackness meant I felt my Blackness every day. I attended a protest calling for justice for Trayvon Martin because what happened in that Florida courtroom was anything but. Still, I'd had the audacity to hope for a different outcome. For change. Even after witnessing how Trayvon's friend Rachel Jeantel was treated on the stand and in the news. She was on the phone with him on the last night of his life. That courtroom and our nation looked at her grief and called it an attitude.

I posted a photo of my sign online before I left my apartment. It read, "1 BLACK MAN IS MURDERED BY POLICE OR VIGILANTES EVERY 28 HOURS IN AMERICA—Will someone you love be next?" In the two days George Zimmerman's lawyer spent haranguing Rachel Jeantel, another Trayvon Martin would be murdered. Another Rachel Jeantel would be broken. The picture of that sign comes up in my Facebook memories every year, followed and preceded by posts about Sandra Bland and Oscar Grant.

Soon after that verdict, I went to the theater to see *Fruitvale Station*. The movie is based on the final day of Oscar Grant's life and what happened to him on New Year's Day 2009, in the early morning hours that felt like they still belonged to the night before. The dawning of a year that much of America wanted to believe was the start of a post-racial era. Obama was a symbol of our country's change, but Grant was proof that change had yet to arrive for Black Americans.

The theater I saw the movie in was unusually small, maybe five short rows of seats. At the end of the credits, I stood. My heart adjusted to what I'd just seen, and my eyes adjusted to the lights coming up. I was the only Black person in the audience. It was as if everyone was looking at me, as if my presence was an epilogue to Black tragedy.

When I got back to my apartment complex, a white man stopped to hold open the door from the garage and said, "You look so sad; is everything OK?" He was compassionate. I told him about the movie. He said he'd never heard of Oscar Grant. I, too, wanted to live in a world where I didn't know the name Oscar Grant. A world where Oscar Grant was still alive and anonymous. A world where neither his life nor his death was a headline.

I remembered Obama being pained as he addressed the nation after the George Zimmerman verdict: he must pause, hands pressed flat against the podium before him; lift his head toward the skies; and close his eyes to keep from crying. Warm light shining on his cheeks. How could he talk about this unbearable weight? The weight of a 5'11" Black seventeen-year-old boy. The weight of a nation of Black boys and girls, women and men, and nonbinary folks he cannot keep safe. We cannot utter Obama's name like a protection spell or pull him over our hearts like a bulletproof vest. A Black president is not an invincibility cloak, after all.

But when I rewatched Obama's July 2013 address, it didn't play out like it did in my memory. The *Washington Post*'s video is the longest, at just over eighteen minutes. It showed Obama entering the room, big grin, laughing. He was bantering with the reporters. This was business, but it was friendly. Everything looked faded, maybe by time, maybe by the bleach-white lighting in the White House press room. Behind him were the White House emblem and an American flag, from which two red-white-and-blue cords dangled.

This was his second statement on the George Zimmerman acquittal, and he was visibly choosing his words with great caution. A Black president cannot talk recklessly about race in America or get too real; each word required a degree of removal, a down-throttling of emotion to ease white viewers. And that was who Obama was addressing.

In my memory, he was consoling Black America, reckoning with the limitations of his power to protect us. But actually, he was serving as a go-between. It's an explainer video seeking to make Black America's pain and righteous rage palatable for white Americans who've just flipped away from Fox News or cut off Rush Limbaugh to judge what Obama had to say about Trayvon.

Throughout much of his campaign, as well as his presidency, Obama asked white Americans to look past his Blackness. But in that moment, he was required to ask that they look directly at it, to see him as a Black man and consider what that meant about his experience as an American. Did they fear what they saw? It's said that this speech was the trip wire that set in motion the Trump presidency because Obama dared to say, "You know, when Trayvon Martin was first shot, I said that this could have been my son. Another way of saying that is Trayvon Martin could have been me 35 years ago."

❤

2016: great year for Trump, trash year for Minda.

After graduate school, I'd moved back home to Louisville to live with my mom while I relaunched my life as a writer. When I'd decided to return to the South, I'd been confident that Hillary Clinton would win the presidency. I knew she was deeply disliked—whether justly or unjustly is debatable—but Trump as president seemed implausible.

When the news presented him as having a chance, I reminded myself these were the same outlets that, four years earlier, had needlessly stirred up our doubts around a second Obama term. Even in Kentucky, where, while driving around town, I witnessed full-size Trump flags waving from the beds of pickup trucks and elderly white men, the sunburn across their cheeks as red as the MAGA hats on their heads, gripping Trump signs at high-traffic intersections, I still refused to accept the possibility Hillary might lose.

But after the election was called, I was reminded of Obama's words from eight years earlier: "America is a place where all things are possible."

In 2020, it was a young Black woman with a cell phone who captured a video of an officer kneeling on the neck of George Floyd, pressing his last breath from him. Protests were set off around the world. In Louisville, the surge of signs that filled the streets bore Breonna Taylor's name. The night they murdered her, the Louisville Metro Police Department had secured a no-knock warrant to search Breonna's home for drugs, implying that there were drugs in her apartment, that there was good reason to believe there would be. There were not and there was not.

The white commenters on news articles about Breonna found little compassion for her. They believed she deserved to have her home raided because a past boyfriend had dealt drugs. If that were the case, I would have been murdered at sixteen and then again at twenty-eight for dating my pot farmer neighbor in Denver. But I wasn't. Instead, I was a college professor, a person who these white commenters paid thousands to so I could teach their children about writing and subtext and knowing what words meant. Like how what they really meant was that Breonna deserved to die for being Black, for being a woman, and for living in the wrong zip code.

I did not immediately join the protests. I attended a demonstration and a march organized by my university and a gathering of spiritual leaders in a park. But I was not among the swarms of people who stayed in the streets, demanding justice. I was afraid of COVID. I was afraid I couldn't walk for miles; I was afraid I was in no shape to run from the police, who were using tear gas, pepper spray, and rubber bullets on protestors. I stayed inside.

I donated money directly to activists and grassroots organizations. I bought supplies, collected them from my friends, and delivered them to my baby sister, who was putting together care packages for activists. It didn't feel like enough. I wanted to be told that it was enough. For days, I listened to the uninterrupted sound of helicopters slicing through the air over my home. Only my guilt was more constant.

There are so many photos of Breonna Taylor. Her with her girls. Her with her man. Her with her family. Her in the same poses, making the same faces my friends and I made in our twenties. Her needing her outfit to be seen. Her needing to be seen. The birthday dress. The hallway strut. That angle that works every time. With Breonna, there's this ever-present sense of more life. But we know the truth. They took her. At some point, the days since her death will outpace the photos and videos and social media posts, the digital remnants of her life.

The pandemic had stretched into several months of 2020 by the time I began my daily walks to Waterfront Park along the Ohio River in Louisville. The college courses I was teaching had gone fully online. The most I walked each day was from my bedroom to my desk, stationed near my front door, or over to my middle sister's house next door. Everyone in my family has been blessed with ankles that ain't shit, and while I'd been fortunate not to have sprained one of mine in a few years, I became concerned my lack of physical activity was going to give an ankle good cause to give out on me. So, I started walking.

Pre-pandemic, the thought of strange men bothering me was generally enough for me to grab my keys and drive wherever I needed to be. Sometimes, I'd be in the car for just a few blocks, even though I rented in this super-gentrified part of the city for its "walkability." But in the pandemic, I had rules for my walks to keep me safe. To reduce street harassment, I never walked at night, and I went out early in the morning if possible. Headphones on. I didn't react when a passing car honked—it was likely a man leering at me.

It was April. The weather was pleasant. On my morning walks, I grew increasingly comfortable being out and about in my neighborhood. I knew many of my neighbors. We waved. We hollered pleasantries across the street. I felt looked out for where I'd once only felt surveilled by strange men. I listened to podcasts. I appreciated the shifting shades of green in the trees, the moss, and the wildflowers along my multiple routes. Sometimes, instead of walking to the river, I did a big loop through the neighborhoods and took note of the New Orleans–style shotgun houses with handmade "Justice for Breonna Taylor" signs in their windows. I walked all spring, summer, and fall, then stopped once winter came to Louisville because I hate the cold.

But on the final day of January 2021, and almost a year into the pandemic, I decided I hated being indoors more. It was not even forty degrees outside, but I found that my earmuffs, tights, and a sweater dress under my oversize raincoat kept me plenty warm. I gave myself the errand of walking a stack of trendy black surgical masks a mile or so to my baby sister's house.

It felt good to move my body, and to see the familiar trees from earlier walks in their winter bareness. On my walk back, a man slowed his car, pulled up alongside me. I knew the rules. I did not look at him.

I was more annoyed than afraid. Men do this to me regularly. He drove ahead and pulled over again. He rolled down his window. He wasn't wearing a mask. He said something to me. I couldn't hear him; I had my AirPods in. I gave him a disgusted look and kept walking. I watched him pull off, drive through the light, and park again. I snapped a photo of his license plate and made an annoyed Instagram Story post about how I was going to have to switch up my route home because this man was being a nuisance.

We were on a one-way street, so I cut through the neighborhood to my right. He circled the block. I should have gone left. I saw him drive by me several times. He didn't appear to be paying me any mind. I started to wonder if he was lost, if he'd been trying to ask me for directions, if I thought the worst of this young Black man for no reason. I deleted my Instagram Story post and kept walking. I let it go.

A block from my home, I stopped. The man's gray Dodge Charger was parked in the lot ahead. He'd continued to follow me, and I hadn't noticed. I hadn't been vigilant enough. For twenty minutes, he'd stalked me from one neighborhood to the next. I'd been lost in a meditative state on my walk. Maybe I was thinking about this book. Figuring out how to write about the never-ceasing terror of men. How the terror is present always, never past.

I had not been drunk on a dance floor in almost a year. It was late afternoon. Broad daylight. A bleak winter Sunday. I was not wearing anything worth seeing. I did not want to be seen. And still, here was this man. Here was this terror.

I didn't run. I didn't change my route again. I didn't call anyone. I just kept walking forward. It was one of those moments with a pervasive sense of the inevitable. Since I was twelve years old, men have been harassing me on the street. They pull over. They turn around in the middle of the road. They block traffic. They holler things. They spit at me. They call me a bitch. The police say they can't do anything unless one of these men touches me.

But men touch me, too. They put their hands up my dress in bars. They let the backs of their hands graze my ass as they pass. They place a hand on the small of my back. My waist. My hips. My arms. My hair. Men with power. Politicians. Start-up founders. Gynecologists. Educators. Men without power who follow me on the street. Down aisles at Target. At the gas station. Corner me on the steps of my own home. On college campuses. On public transportation. Men pushing their possessions along in a shopping cart. Because any man can reign over a woman unattended. Any man.

Even this man.

I walked with intention. Head up. Almost home. He got out of the car. He opened his passenger door. Past became present. Every act of terror I'd endured stacked one on top of the other. It was the same man again and again. The same fear repeated and survived. But I believed this was the day I would die. That he would pull me into the car. That he would have a gun. That he would shoot me. That I could not protect my body. That I could not save myself.

So, what happened, what actually happened, when I walked by him was both anticlimactic and traumatic because all that was in his hand was his dick. Had I known it would not be a gun, I wouldn't have even looked at him. Jacking off at me would just be one more thing I risk men doing to me when I leave my home. I would be thankful that at least I'd been wearing my raincoat. But because I believed this man was going to shoot me, because I looked him directly in the eyes, because my pulse seized, this became more than just one more thing, one more man.

Later, I joked that I wondered why I didn't hop into his car. He'd left the keys in the ignition and had his pants around his ankles. He was in no condition to chase after me. I imagined aloud for my friends; I described him stumbling over his jeans, falling, getting asphalt burns on his penis, just lying there in pain while I did donuts in the parking lot, whooping and hollering at the perverse absurdity of the men who wished to harm me because I had the audacity to be something they wanted but could not have. Violence as spectacle.

But I did not joyride. I ran into traffic to cross the street. I called my middle sister, who lives next door to me. I was crying, and she appeared outside on the corner, looking up the street for me. She ushered me into her house, and I sat with her and her husband while I gathered myself.

Then, she walked me back home once we were certain the man was no longer waiting for me, no longer watching me.

I did not feel comfortable calling the police and giving them the description of a Black man in a hoodie in a predominantly Black neighborhood. This man had put me in the position of weighing my own safety against the safety of every Black man in my community. This is the double bind of misogyny and racism.

Not that my concern made a difference. The next day, once I'd gathered as much information as I could in an attempt to be certain the wrong Black man wouldn't be bothered, I called my local precinct, and I was transferred to a detective. He was kind but apologetic. This was not considered a sex crime. It's such a low-level offense, he said, that the most they could do, even if they caught this man, was attempt to scare him into not doing it again. His right to whip his dick out in public is more protected than my right to move my body around unaccosted.

I've had encounters with the police. An officer who pulled me over in Brownsville, Texas, and demanded to know whether or not I was an American. An officer in Orange County who found it hard to believe that I owned the car I was driving. An officer who refused to believe I hadn't been drinking when he pulled me over just outside of a nightclub parking lot. He made me get out of the car and grilled me for so long, I nearly had to beg him to just go on and give me a Breathalyzer test so I could leave. And somehow, the insistence of the police that they couldn't protect me from this man was almost more upsetting than any of those other encounters.

When I posted about my experience on Facebook and Instagram, I received dozens of comments, texts, DMs, emails, and phone calls. So many women, queer, and nonbinary folks shared with me their similar experiences. For some, the stalking and exposure went on for months. Most of the people who messaged me said seeing me speak out had helped them, that they never shared what had happened to them: What right did they have to be distraught about something so common?

We are not to blame for the terrors of men. Or the terrors of this American dream. A Black president hadn't made it any safer for me to be Black in America than feminism has made it safe for me to be a woman in America.

When Kamala Harris announced her presidential campaign, I did not allow myself the same audacious hope I'd held for Barack Obama. As a nation, we were a decade older, a decade deeper into the sorrow over the limitations of what a Black president could and could not do for Black people in America. To look like us was no longer enough. To be first was no longer the threshold.

On Twitter, my feed was full of references to Harris as "Top Cop." Her record as California state attorney general was rightfully scrutinized. Abolitionists questioned how anyone could chant "Defund the Police" while donating funds to Harris's campaign. And yet when I looked at her, listened to her sound bites from the debates, I saw and heard an accomplished Black woman, and I had to question whether or not we were unfairly asking her to carry what we'd neglected to place on Obama, to be accountable for some of our heartache and loss. It wouldn't be the first time a mule was made of a Black woman.

Even though I thought I was ambivalent about Harris, on November 7, when she walked toward the podium to give her acceptance speech as vice president-elect of the United States, I discovered that I'd been nurturing a secret, unacknowledged hope for Harris. There is no other way to explain my tears.

I, too, am a multiracial Black woman, a daughter of an immigrant, an auntie. Whether I acknowledged it or not, I saw myself in Harris. I think often about how challenging it is to be upwardly mobile in this country without contributing to the oppression of someone else. How almost any amount of or method to achieve financial security comes at the expense and casual exploitation of others. To overcome the odds and find success within the system is to still be of the system. How different is the machine behind a politician from the one behind a corporate salesperson? A professor? A writer? All positions that have paid my bills. Have given me clout in our society. Have validated me. To become aware in my midthirties that the hard-fought successes I've gained in my career may not be the accomplishments that I think they are—that maybe I've strived for the wrong achievements—is a hard awareness to reckon with.

But it's not too late to imagine more for my life and other possibilities for this nation. Just as I imagined more for myself than racist managers and shaky employment in the wake of the Great Recession at the age of twenty-three. Now, nearing forty, my cloud of Obama euphoria may have dissipated, but my audacity of hope remains.

Chapter 19

Epilogue

I want a millennial *Waiting to Exhale*. Give me Keke Palmer changing the password to her billionaire boyfriend's crypto wallet after she learns, ten years into their relationship, that his ethically nonmonogamous marriage isn't so ethical after all. When he calls to rage at her, she drops her iPhone—no case, neon acrylics—from the rolled-down window of her Mercedes-Benz G-Wagon into traffic on the 405, and a motorcycle splicing lanes races over it, cracks the screen; the boyfriend's screams dissolve into static. Give me Michaela Jaé Rodriguez behind the wheel of a bulldozer headed directly into the side of her husband's love shack in the woods, a cabin he built by hand while she spent weekends ferrying the kids between relatives and extracurricular activities in an SUV crossover she's hated since the day they bought it. Make certain the sound of the logs splintering, snapping, collapsing is distinct, that there is a shot of her stilettos sinking into a bed of russet pine needles when she leaps, light as can be, from the heavy machinery. Give me SZA in her acting debut. The quiet one. Put a tattoo gun in her hand. Show us how she covers up the looping letters of an ex-lover's name, the curlicues that were meant to manifest forever love, and makes them into heartbreak art—a flower, a tree, a bird—something that would never hurt you.

How she fills in faces, shades them into geometry, into analog Tetris pieces, into anything but a reminder that believing in forever and actually living it are rarely ever the same thing. As she sits on one of those tiny stools and crouches over a client, show the hem of her skirt rising, the tattoo on her thigh in homage to the One she never speaks of; then pan the camera, show that one entering the studio, the old-school door chimes shimmering in sound over their head. Give me Lizzo leading a sing-along of "Truth Hurts"; the girls on her yacht, weaves streaming in the breeze, backs as arched as full sails, like a remixed *Titanic* moment, are the queens of their own world. The women have decided to release their woes, spend the summer island-hopping. Dress Lizzo in a white captain's hat that has more fabric than her string bikini, and the man who brings out the refreshments should have almost as much sparkle as the champagne he hands to each of the friends before whispering something in Lizzo's ear that just makes her grin. Over his shoulder, she sees a yacht full of hotties approaching; her girls see it, too. Everything's gonna be OK. At least for a little bit because even though it's next to impossible to meet the right person, the next person who wants to waste your time will always be along shortly. A millennial *Waiting to Exhale* ends with new love on the horizon instead of self-actualization? Leave it alone. They're setting us up for the sequel. I want that, too.

I want to watch the millennial *Waiting to Exhale* alone, pressing the back of my head into the plush velvet of a classic movie theater seat, no vomit-colored leather, no automated reclining. I want a big bag of popcorn and the no-you-really-shouldn't-believe-it's-butter to glom beneath my nails. I want to regret not paying for an overpriced Sierra Mist. I want to wonder, when the movie hits a lull midway through, if I should have used the money I spent on a ticket to pay for Bumble premium instead because clearly, their free services are not going to help me move my love life along. I want to snack and space out to the millennial *Waiting to Exhale* as I nurse another micro-heartbreak bestowed upon me by a man who couldn't do the basics, like ask you *"what your interests are, who you be with, things that make you smile"*—Biggie put it to a beat, and these motherfuckers still can't remember the simplest shit. I want the feel-good reminder that even when these men fail me—again and again—I'll always have my girls, just like Molly and Issa on a couch on the curb in *Insecure*.

I want to leave the theater and remember how smart I am for parking near the side door and exit into the sunlight, soothed and ready for another round of disappointing dating roulette. I want to pull out of the parking lot and pray that the millennial *Waiting to Exhale* has filled me with enough hopefulness to prop me up until the next heartbreak knocks me down.

I don't want to drive home and worry that the millennial *Waiting to Exhale* isn't enough to keep me going. That I need more than the love of good friends to be content. And I don't want to wonder whether or not I should feel guilty about admitting it. That I fantasize about meeting the love of my life and disappearing into him, my default source of human interaction.

I'm done with heartbreak. Even the small ones. Micro-heartbreaks are like Skittles. They may appear different, but they're all the same flavor. The man who goes ghost in the middle of the best banter you've had all year is the one who reveals he's an anti-vaxxer three dates in, is the one who was already devastatingly cruel to a woman you know. These are not the major heartbreaks that trigger month-long crying jags. The ones your friends take you out for drinks over. No, these are the ones you only regret because you told your friends about them too soon. One more wrecked fantasy. These little tears are only enough to ruin your morning. To momentarily mistake the ding of a fully charged phone for the "sweet dreams, beautiful" text you've received for less than two weeks. The memory of these *petites morts* adds a dash of melancholy to your Tuesday.

A Skittle is a little thing, but have enough of them, an entire bag of them, and sugar becomes grit. Expect sweet; get decay. Your stomach churns. You won't remember these inconsequential men in a few years, but you're not quite as ready to forget them as you appear to your friends. You make a show of laughing off their small slights. You move on quickly because they expect you to, because what is three dates, really? But it's not just three dates; it's one date, two dates, three dates a dozen times. It's disappointment scattered, covered, and smothered. But it's not even like you want the compassion of your friends. You want to release these men, too. Be done with them just like that. You, too, are tired of your own minute heartbreaks. But what are you supposed to do with the minor aches? They resurface repeatedly, like pennies you keep forgetting to spend in your cup holder, sticky and pointless but still in rotation, still a physical object, still a reminder.

When you're perpetually single, it's easier to point to what's missing than what you have. It's my bed that's filled with things that are not the body of a lover—books, clothes, laptop. The food packaged in twos and fours at the grocery store. It's credit card companies pestering you to add a second person to your account—"Double your cashback rewards!"—the assumption being that you share your finances with someone instead of managing every bill, every month, on your own. How you smile when your dual-income friends announce they've bought a home. It's the dinner parties, trips, and couples-only outings—not that anyone excludes their single pals directly; the absence of an invitation to the evening you watch in ten-second installments on your friends' Instagram Stories speaks for itself. I don't begrudge my loved ones the inherent satisfaction in even numbers, everyone tidily partnered, their human security blankets within arm's reach. But being single is not just being the odd one out; you're even less. An unpartnered person is like zero—the physical representation of nothing. Apparently, our solo presence is incapable of adding anything to certain occasions. Even in death, we aren't granted a reprieve from our single status, soulmates certain they'll be reunited in heaven, lovingly chattering about past lives spent together—get ready for third-wheeling in the afterlife. Or maybe not. Maybe your favorite duo will ask you to make them a trio.

Dating apps are overrun with couples looking for a third. Everyone's some configuration or another of ethically nonmonogamous. I'm now expected to learn to share someone's perfect somebody when I've yet to have my own. I describe myself as emotionally conservative, sexually liberal. I can't imagine maintaining multiple emotional connections while simultaneously needing to manage my own jealousy and competitiveness. If I joined this wave of nonmonogamy, I'd have to figure out a new way of being in love when I've barely figured out one-to-one romantic relationships. It's not fair that the world's moving on without me. I'm trying not to be bitter about it, but I'm tired of being denied what I feel owed. *Is this how white people who voted for Trump feel?*

On the patio of a Mexican restaurant, a Corona-branded umbrella cast its shade over C and me. Occasionally, one of us would tip back in our chair and let the sun warm our face, kiss life into our soul. It was a farewell lunch. C has lived all over the world. Next up: Mumbai. She'd been home for a year—twelve straight months of disappointing dating. But that isn't even close to being the record for a Black woman in the Bluegrass State. I'd already been let down in love for twice the amount of time she had. And while I pinned most of my romance woes on location, I knew from living in Cincinnati, LA, and Denver that lonely feels the same in any city.

But what C has on me is age. She's already in her forties. Each decade a woman enters into without a committed life partner, the further people's views shift from seeing her as someone unlucky in love to someone who is deeply flawed—it's your choices, your standards, your looks. And it's not just other people; you begin to do it, too, swapping unlucky with unloved, with unwanted, with un-fuck-wit-able. This ageism persists even though human beings are living longer. Even though the average marriage only lasts eight years. This means the odds of anyone spending a lifetime in love with the same person is unlikely (but obviously, there are relationships that stay the course). So, why can't we normalize finding "your person" after you've found yourself? Your twenties are for floundering. Your thirties are for figuring it out. And your forties, your forties could be for falling in love. Having children does become more complicated on this timeline, but people have been making it work. Besides, I don't want to have a baby, and neither does C.

Over lunch, I described the most recent episode of *This Is Us*. The one where Beth tells Randall she loves him and she has no regrets, but loving him and living inside his dream have come at the expense of living hers. She's pushed her dance dreams to the side for his career aspirations and their children. I challenged C, and myself, to consider which stretch of our lives we'd exchange for steady love. It was hard for each of us to say.

C squeezed a wedge of lime over her tacos and contemplated my question. The tangy scent of the citrus lifted into the air briefly. Dark sunglasses concealed her eyes.

I tend to imagine that the partner I am missing out on is the partner who would have been the best possible match for me. The missing partner is not the partner who would have dragged me down into debt. Not the partner determined to decimate my self-esteem. Not the one who'd be reluctant to hold me in bed. I rarely imagine that my singleness has saved me from the misery that loves company. The worst possible partner wouldn't be worth trading for any portion of my life—but they would garner me an invite to the next couples' brunch.

Still, even when imagining the best possible partner, the question I asked C is hard to answer. How much would I wager for a never-ending love with the right man? I've believed I was ready for a relationship since I left my last serious one at twenty-three. Had I met my man at twenty-three, it's likely nothing that's happened to me beyond that age would have happened, or at least it would have looked drastically different. Would I be willing to never have made the friends I made that year? The women who held me together through heartbreak and my hair back in the aftermath of too much partying?

Maybe twenty-three would have been too soon. What about twenty-seven? I was living in LA then. If I'd met my man and he'd wanted to stay in that city forever—perhaps he had family nearby or his career was location specific—could I have spent the rest of my life as an Angeleno? The waifs, the traffic, life teetering on the verge of the Big One. I don't know.

At twenty-eight, I was living in Denver. It's a city I think I could have been happy in if I'd moved there already married. It wasn't a city meant for meeting someone, at least not for me or any of the Black women I socialized with. But a husband and I could have had a happy little life at the base of a mountain. But is that really true? Am I a wife who'd participate in winter sports and hikes through tick-filled forests? Would I have even become a writer if I hadn't been free to flee that city for an MFA program in the desert? I don't know. Maybe my husband would have followed me, or maybe my life would have followed the *This Is Us* script, and like Beth and her dance dreams, mine would have been indefinitely deferred.

When I moved home to Louisville at thirty-one, I was ready to settle down, even if it meant settling. I found me a tall, good-looking man. I was patient with him, gently explaining how a story he'd told me was transphobic or how his take on some movie was misogynistic. Still, his feelings bruised. There was tension when he found out I'd only walked his dog for twenty minutes instead of an hour because it was dark out and the temperature was in the twenties. He didn't read. I didn't watch sports. But whatever, I was ready to shift my life into its final phase, for everything to be decided. Unfortunately, there was another girl. She waited until my birthday to comment on an Instagram photo of him and me. He'd been trying to convince me to move to Cleveland, where he planned to live with his mother and go to grad school. I refused to relocate, and he insisted we could make it work long distance. Loving that man would have meant spending vacation days and expendable income traveling back and forth to fucking Ohio. I DM'd her—she could have him. I'd learned over the years that I could survive heartbreak, but that was only because I always had my own life to return to. If I'd put my life on pause to settle for that man, I don't know how I'd manage the disappointment when the relationship inevitably fell apart.

That man was a cheater, but now, I'm in my late thirties, and I've ended relationships with men who I believe would have remained faithful and intended to marry me. But they were asking me to live in their dreams with them at a time when my own dreams—like this book—were becoming more possible. One man dreamed of us in a renovated Victorian home with a pattern inset in the wood floors. But he was mid-divorce, and when I looked at him, I wondered if every moment we spent together was a rehash. Us standing in the kitchen together, side by side, following the lines of a recipe. That look, that touch. If that falling-too-fast feeling was a by-product of his rush to replace someone else. If when I spoke certain words, they rippled in his memory, made his heart ache for her. Whether I was trying to find love along the scar of his broken marriage.

Another one sat beside me near a firepit, and his facade of compromise fell away. "I want it all," he said. Our all-inclusive life meant children, meant me leaving my city, meant me deprioritizing my career to support the family we'd have. I watched the flames of the fire lick the air and knew I would burn that relationship down before I made kindling of my dreams—and I did. I've never wanted children. I need a life I can fold up like an origami swan and float away with when necessary. Children are the opposite of that, forever unfolding.

I wanted so much of what these partners were offering, but I just couldn't jump the rails and send my life down an entirely different track. When is a man your destiny, and when is he a distraction? Undecided.

By the end of lunch, our to-go boxes packed, C hadn't offered an answer to my question, and neither had I. We hugged goodbye, then parted ways, headed in opposite directions, on our own as we navigated around couples holding hands, strolling down the sidewalk.

When I left Louisville in my early twenties, I didn't know that my life would look so drastically different from the lives of my high school and college friends who'd stayed behind. Most people never step out of the life they were born into. Leaving broadens what's possible; it's cozying up to the unknown and welcoming the unpredictable.

I frequently question how this tragic love life could happen to me. *Whyyy meeee?* But did it happen to me, or did I choose it? At every moment of my life that asked me to choose, I chose the path that led me further from the marriage I claimed I wanted. I left the South, where the marriage rates (and the divorce rates) are higher. I ended a long-term relationship with a man whose love was most devout. I chose career. I chose grad school. I chose assholes. I say I was ready for another serious relationship at twenty-three, but I didn't narrow my dating pool to serious men only. I dated the ones who lit up something inside me, men who detonated my heart. The slackers, the artists, the ones selfish about living out their dreams. The ones I wished I could be more like. If you insist on loving men who can't commit, how committed are you to commitment? It's possible to be perpetually single without being perpetually heartbroken, but that was not the path I chose.

None of those men ever asked me to marry them. I think they knew I couldn't be trusted. That there was no way I could remain what I'd presented myself as, that at some point, I would stop acquiescing, stop holding my breath around them. I can't fault them for recognizing the largeness of the life I wanted to live, my ambitions beyond playing the supporting cast in their dreams. I had to get honest with myself about wanting to be my own main character. And equally important, I wanted to be with a man who didn't require that I lie to myself about who he was.

My best friend from high school, S, is divorced. It was difficult. Her children were young at the time. She's remarried now. Her husband is open to adventure, kind, and cares about her happiness. I like him for her. I admire her for having the strength to choose the life she wanted.

For work, S was driving back and forth between Kentucky and Florida every few weeks. We shared hours-long phone calls with topics that spanned the length of our friendship. On one call, I was taking a rare—for me—hike through the woods in southern Indiana while we chatted about the "miserable women" literature we'd been assigned to read in high school. I told her, as the trail led me back toward the parking lot and my car, "I'll never forget what a downer the end of *The Awakening* was." I remember, as a teenager, being disgusted that the protagonist just straight up marches into the ocean.

Why were our syllabi filled with books about unfulfilled women? My bestie quipped, "This is our canon?"

It was early March. The trees were still bare. A narrow creek burbled, and a misplaced foot meant sliding a sneaker into fudgy mud. My Apple Watch dinged happily when my green exercise ring closed and then again when my magenta activity ring was completed.

We read the stories of centuries of women who could not find freedom within their marriages. But it wasn't like there were counter-narratives of women who were single and joyful, either. To be alone was to be destitute and ostracized. To be vulnerable. To be cast as a witch. To be branded unworthy. It's not hard to see how women trapped by marriage on the page morphed into women springing their own marriage traps on the big screen. Propaganda to convince us we couldn't be fulfilled without the same marriages that left our foremothers drowning in dissatisfaction. I grew up on movies with women losing men in ten days and winning them back over pickup games of basketball.

I detoured just before the parking lot and ventured a bit down another trail toward what looked like a man-made lake. It was small and unimpressive. I headed back to my car.

If I have to continue this life unpaired, is it too much to ask for some positive representation? Where are the women who see their aloneness as solitude? I want to see women who have actively chosen a life of one. Women who are still open to love but are passing their time pleasantly without desperation. Women who don't scramble toward any bit of cast-off attention from a man, women who are choosing themselves without question. Always. What if instead of wading into a watery death, Kate Chopin's heroine dove beneath the waves, grew gills, and swam through to a true awakening on the shore of an island of Amazons? What if her happily ever after became a good book; a warm mug of tea; and the wet, green scent of spring flowing through a nearby open window, her children gone for the weekend?

But women in the books we were assigned to read were very different from the women in the books I found on my own. Janie walking out of homes where love no longer resided. Sula opting out of the dull norms and drudgery expected of the women in her town. And the Black women writers behind these books who were equally emblematic of the life I could live. Instead of a life that swung back and forth between love found and love lost, my art could be my central passion, the community of women around me my most important love affair.

I stayed on the phone with my bestie my entire drive back across the river to Louisville and until I was inside, about to strip down for my shower. I wished S a safe rest of her road trip before I hung up. Sometimes, it's as if her life is the path I didn't choose. We'd both dated our high school sweethearts past college. While I moved to California with mine, she'd stayed in Louisville with hers. They were engaged at one point. When she called me about their breakup, I knew my own was soon to follow. I remember listening to her tell me why they were done for good this time while I lay on my back on the diving board in my ex's grandparents' backyard, staring straight up at Orange County blue skies, chlorine and orange blossoms in the air. Kentucky was so far away.

When she married her first husband, I flew home for her wedding on an Indiana farm. I missed her first pregnancy, but I felt the miracle of tiny feet kick her belly from within when she was pregnant with her second child. While I was in grad school on the West Coast, I'd come home from the bar and she'd call me, three time zones away, and we'd sit on the phone together, her breast pump whirring in the background of my drunk murmuring. Later, after grad school, I moved back home to Louisville. During her divorce, I was there for the texts and the calls, and the drinks and the nights spent out too late, as if we could snatch back a bit of the youth the years had taken from us. Now, she is married again, happy again.

And still, I'm single. No children. On what must be my fourth career. Why does a sense of inertia cling to that word? *Single.* As if I've not lived a life, too. As if, on those calls with my best friend, she wasn't consoling and guiding me as well, through heartbreak and moves across states and big risks. She granted my narrative the same sovereignty as hers. And her life looking more conventional hadn't insulated her from heartbreak or loneliness. Pain is pain, joy is joy, and you're bound to encounter them both, no matter which series of life choices you make.

I am thankful all those men I dated were unanswered prayers. When I was a child, I loved catching lightning bugs. I'd put dozens in a single glass jar and place it on my dresser, watching the magical blinking all night until I fell asleep. Every morning, my father made me release the lightning bugs back into our yard. I'd plead with him to let me keep them, but he insisted that they belonged in their world, not mine. The men I've loved were like those lightning bugs; they flickered beautifully briefly, but once cupped in my hands, they dimmed and became nothing special. They were meant to light up moments of my life, then be released. It's the women in my life who have held a steady glow for me.

The drive from my home to K's home is the length of two moderately long pop songs. The year she tells me about the painful lump in her breast—so big she can see it through her skin, like a chunk of Kryptonite embedded in her chest, throbbing—I listen to Panic! at the Disco's new song "High Hopes" on endless loop in my car. She is thirty-five.

The weekend between her biopsy and receiving the results from her doctor, she asks me to have a drink with her. We do that short-girl clamber onto two stools at the bar. It's a crowded venue that was designed to look like a series of living rooms. "This may be my last drink for a while," she says, raising her glass of bourbon in the air, tapping it against mine, then against the bar before bringing it to her lips.

It's cancer.

But her husband is the exact husband you would want by your side during cancer. During lunch at a restaurant with a patio that overlooks the Ohio River, rolling murky and brown, K tells me about the women in her cancer Facebook groups who've discovered, over the course of their illnesses, that they do not have the husbands you would want by your side during cancer, not even close. Husbands who still expect their chemo-choked wives to solely manage the children and the home. Husbands who look at their wives' changing bodies and the changes to come with disappointment. Husbands who check out and hope to check back in when their wives return to the right side of healthy. But K's husband is pure love, pure patience, and his only want from any of this is for his wife not to die at fucking thirty-five years old—the state of her tits in "the After" is irrelevant.

She's planned our lunch around her chemo schedule so she can enjoy her food without nausea and the delicate spring weather blooming all around us. We decide to treat ourselves to a few ounces of crab off the raw menu. As she talks, I am happy for her, happy that she married well. I am, but I am also something else. Something harder to admit. It's bad form to be jealous of your friend battling cancer.

I couldn't help but think about what it'd be like if I were the one stricken with breast cancer at an abnormally young age. Who would be there to care for me? I imagined myself alone in my gold-framed canopy bed, dehydrated, silently praying for someone to bring me a glass of water, gingerly lifting myself out of bed and creeping into the kitchen to pour my own. On that patio with K, I'm convinced that as a single person, I'd be just as in it by myself as one of those Facebook group wives.

We've been taught that a spouse is someone to care for you when you're old. A husband as an illness contingency plan isn't the most romantic thing, but when I catalog my fears around never finding my right partner, dealing with aging and poor health alone is a frightening future. But is it more frightening than being married to a man who refuses to honor the "in sickness and in health" portion of our vows? Do I really need to be frightened at all?

When my cousin gets their gender-affirming surgeries, their friends call and visit and feed them and stay with them until they are well enough to care for themselves. They are there, unlike the supposedly obligated husbands who are not. When that man stalked me through my neighborhood, my friends and family reached out immediately, sent cards and flowers and left baked goods on my steps, did what they could to care for me. Even with K, even with the exact husband you'd want by your side during cancer, there's no way he could be all the things she needed without the support of her community. When he travels for work, we walk the dog; we stay with K; we are less than a phone call away. There is no point in our lives that our needs aren't too much for one person to handle. Even love does not somehow make it possible for one person to be our everything. Maybe I'm a little more nonmonogamous than I thought—at least in my friendships.

K's love is the sticky, grippy kind of love that isn't afraid to make itself known. Once she is cancer-free, her hair grows back in layers of baby-soft curls that sweep over one another in brown waves, a tender ocean providing cover.

We cannot say whether our partner will stay if we become ill. Or if our health will return in full or at all. We cannot know if our community will be there for us, in the short term or the long. K and I have discussed how you can't make the choices you make based on the outcomes you can't predict. All we can do is love ourselves, love others, and hope to be loved in return.

It's been more than a decade since my last long-term relationship. I consider myself to have mostly spent my adult life single, but I'm not sure that that's actually true. I can't just write off all those short-term, revolving-door relationships. It's not a failure to leave a situation that is no longer working. Maybe my romantic relationships are so short because, in my experience, it's been much easier to be happy without a man than it has been to be happy with a man. This isn't a knock against men, not completely. Aside from compatibility issues, to love a man is to bring the patriarchy into your private life. I don't want to be mansplained to at the office and in the bedroom. I don't want to experience the gender wage gap at work and the gender labor gap over household chores. I gripe that I pay every bill by myself, but I've also been fortunate to be able to pay every bill by myself. I've never had to compromise on my feelings in the name of financial stability. Maybe I'm foolish to be holding out for a relationship of true equals—*In this patriarchy?*—but at this point, there is too much at stake. In my twenties, it was easier to fall for men who weren't right for me because so much of my life didn't feel right for me. Those men were portals into alternate realities, potentially better realities. I was searching for a man to build a life around, but in my thirties, I'm waiting to find a man who fits the life I've built.

For proof I'm capable of longevity, again, I turn to my friendships. They span decades and multiple states. And for all the real estate I've given dating in my life's story, my friendships are the relationships that taught me how to show care and tenderness, to forgive others and myself. One of my first and closest friends in Orange County was E. She was the first person I knew who saw a therapist, or at least the first one who spoke openly about it. Soon enough, "Well, what did Debbie say about it?" was a regular part of our conversations. Before E, I was the type of person who'd get upset and end a friendship to prove to someone just how much I didn't need them. But these moments didn't seem to register for her. She'd continue to show up at the same time to pick me up for the gym and would keep sending me five-thousand-word emails in the middle of the workday, until I was forced to explain that I was angry at her—tricked into talking about my feelings. After we talked it over, whatever issue I had no longer seemed that serious. In fact, nothing became too big or too small to share with her—or her with me. When I told her, over dinner in a Vietnamese restaurant, that I was leaving California for Colorado, she wept. Whenever I return to Los Angeles, I fly out of Orange County just so I can stay the night with E, curl up on her couch under her fluffy duvet, and sip mugs of tea while we reminisce over our drunk-on-the-dance-floor years.

Having the love of friends does not stop the wanting. And that doesn't make the love from my friends any less valuable. I don't know where a Black woman nearing forty should go to find romantic love. But I do know I don't have to go it alone, that I'm not waiting by myself. I can both want more and appreciate that I already have more love than most in my life. A love that has yet to fail me.

In a millennial *Waiting to Exhale*, just like in the original, the people who choose you, who choose to be by your side, who choose you to be by theirs, are not a consolation prize. They are, and will always be, your greatest love story. The grandest gesture of love. The epilogue to my heartbreak years.

ACKNOWLEDGMENTS

I want to thank all the women of my twenties whom I would not have made it through my heartbreak years without. Thank you to my high school sweetheart for being my safe harbor. Thank you, Women Writing for (a) Change Cincinnati, Lighthouse Writers Workshop, Voices of Our Nations Arts Foundation (VONA), and Storyknife. Kayla for finding me—I owe you a Waffle House night; Kiese for publishing me first and so much more; Sari for scooping me up out of the slush pile at Longreads and the series that followed; Lilly for being the first to invite me to read in NYC; and Alex for being the connect for my first column. Cinelle for her guidance and including me in *A Measure of Belonging*. Laura for believing in this book and making it possible for me to create my own sabbatical year. Lisa Pegram, I hope we get to meet someday, and thank you for your support and your strong, insightful edits. Vidalia for your gentle encouragement in undergrad. Tatyana for the rummy and wine nights in grad school. My writing group—Natassja, Natalie, Asha, Lis, and Edgar—for getting to name-drop them on every panel forever. Susan Straight for treating me like a daughter. Lois for taking me seriously as a writer, despite my age and my dating perils. My Creative Circle—Kaitlyn, Lucie, and Olivia—for just going with it the first time I invited them over to meet each other. Stephanie for being there all along—our friendship is its own kind of memoir. Ewa for her legendary black shorts and always being first on the dance floor with me.

ABOUT THE AUTHOR

Minda Honey's essays on politics and relationships have appeared in the *Los Angeles Review of Books*, the *Washington Post*, the *Guardian*, the *Oxford American*, *Teen Vogue*, and Longreads. She is the editor of Black Joy at Reckon News and was director of the BFA in Creative Writing program at Spalding University, an advice columnist for *LEO Weekly* in Louisville, Kentucky, and founder of the alt-indie publication *TAUNT*. Her work is featured in *Burn It Down: Women Writing about Anger*, *A Measure of Belonging: Twenty-One Writers of Color on the New American South*, and *Sex and the Single Woman: 24 Writers Reimagine Helen Gurley Brown's Cult Classic*. For more information visit www.mindahoney.com.